Historic
NEWFOUNDLAND

Historic NEWFOUNDLAND

Text by
Harold Horwood

◆

Photography by
John de Visser

Toronto
OXFORD UNIVERSITY PRESS
1986

CANADIAN CATALOGUING IN PUBLICATION DATA

De Visser, John, 1930–
   Historic Newfoundland

ISBN 0-19-540564-1

1. Newfoundland — Description and travel — 1981-
Views.* 2. Historic buildings — Newfoundland —
Pictorial works. 3. Newfoundland — History —
Pictorial works. I. Horwood, Harold, 1923–
II. Title.

FC2167.5.D48 1986   971.8'0022'2   C86-094120-5
F1122.D48 1986

Produced by Boulton Publishing Services, Inc.
Designed by Fortunato Aglialoro

1 2 3 4 - 9 8 7 6

Colour separations by
Lasersharp Inc., Toronto

Printed in Hong Kong by
Scanner Art Services, Inc., Toronto

Introduction

THE SWEEP OF HISTORY in Newfoundland has been so much vaster than in any other part of Canada that most Canadians simply ignore it and forget that it ever happened. They still say, in Ontario, "The French were here first," meaning that Canada began with Quebec, never having heard that in Champlain's time the Newfoundland town of Trinity was far more populous, and produced far more wealth, than the whole of New France. And Trinity is merely one instance. One could say it with even greater truth of St. John's, or Harbour Grace, or Carbonear.

Even if you ignore the Norse settlement of A.D. 1005, and confine yourself to what happened after the Cabot voyages, you still find that St. John's was established early in the 1500s, and was an important trading and manufacturing centre with iron founding and ships' chandleries at the time of the Cartier voyages (1534–1541.)

The great figures of Newfoundland include Sir Richard Whitbourne (arrived in Newfoundland in 1579), Sir Humphrey Gilbert (1583), the pirate admiral Captain Peter Easton (1610), John Guy (1610), and Sir David Kirke (1638). Newfoundlanders have never forgotten what most Canadians have never known, that Kirke conquered Quebec exactly one century before General Wolfe was born.

Newfoundlanders have a deeper historical sense, a more intimate knowledge of their past, a folk-memory more fully developed than any other people in Canada. In the towns of Conception Bay they speak of the folk hero Peter Easton as though he had sailed away last year, instead of retiring to the French Riviera to enjoy his wealth in 1614. When I first visited the old settlement of Port-de-Grave, a man leaning on a scythe paused in his haying to say, "John Guy? Oh yes, we mind he well enough. He come sailin' in here in 1610 after all the good harbours was already bespoke, and some of we people told about a pretty fair little cove around the headland there to the south, with nobody fishin', so that's where 'e settled, in Cupids." Howard Morry of Ferryland, who recorded the oral history of his town on tape in the 1960s, knew it in great detail back to the time of his own great-grandmother. Some of Morry's oral history, doubted by the professionals, was later confirmed by documentary research.

Newfoundland history is that of a people struggling against just about everything—storms and ice-fields, pirates and privateers who wanted to rob them of their meagre earnings, Dutch and French raiders sent to wrest their country from them, and last of all, their own "home" government in far-off England, where Newfoundland was regarded not as a suitable place for settlement so much as a massive fishing station to be exploited by the English West Country merchants and the twenty thousand transient fishermen they employed.

In the face of all this Newfoundlanders became as tough and tenacious as Newfoundland dogs. They took their ships' guns behind improvised earth-works and fought off the French navy not once, but many times. They took their hunting muskets and went out to meet a French army in the hills above St. John's. When a New England governor offered to take the people from the Ferryland colony into the safety of his domain they replied proudly that they had three times fought off the King's enemies by their own unaided resources, and were prepared to do the same again.

Little wonder that they rejected Confederation with Canada so vigorously in 1869, when the anti-confederate party won election by a landslide twenty-one seats to nine:

> Hurrah for our own native isle Newfoundland;
> Not a stranger shall hold one inch of her strand!
> Her face turns to Britain, her back to the Gulf;
> Come near at your peril, Canadian wolf!

The miracle was that they ever accepted it at all—even by the slenderest of margins in 1948. But you'd have your work cut out today to find more than a handful of serious anti-confederates in the tenth province. Confederation has given Newfoundland security, and the opportunity for social progress, without doing any real damage to the heritage or the ethos of a people who remain essentially separate from the melting pot of the Mainland. The Newfoundland stores in Toronto attest to separate tastes, the Newfoundland clubs to a separate social structure. Toronto has become "the biggest outport" with some twenty thousand Newfoundlanders ethnically separate from the rest of the city. Newfoundland is the only province with its own pavilion at the Toronto Caravan, an annual international exposition by Toronto's ethnic minorities.

Newfoundland has been described as a rock in the Atlantic inhabited by a race of Irish mystics. A half-truth. Newfoundland is indeed nearly one-third Irish. Newfoundlanders, if not exactly mystics, do at least flavour their toughness with a deep strain of romanticism. Even the contemporary poets have a hard time making their lines sound less like Whitman and more like Atwood. As for artists and prose writers, they are romantics without apology. They write with deep and abiding nostalgia of a land that is half historic childhood and half myth; they paint with a sense of love and compassion, rather than with harsh reality: the magic realists deal deeply in magic, fully convinced that the true reality lies beyond the world of the five senses.

Paradoxically, Newfoundland, while treasuring the past, has always been receptive to change. The fishermen have eagerly embraced each techno-logical change as it has become available. Such an attitude is essential to their livelihood, and has been transferred to other aspects of life. The social revolution of the 1960s and 1970s had a very easy ride in Newfoundland. Apostles of the "new culture" found St. John's far more receptive than most Canadian cities, far less hostile to social change, far more willing to swing with the trends, whatever they might be. Columnist Ray Guy, an enormously popular satirist, who described himself as "certified funny" when he won the Leacock Award, went so far as to say that Newfoundlanders had always been hippies, waiting for the rest of North America to catch up. It is certainly true that things "hang loose" in St. John's and the outports in a way that they certainly do not in Halifax, Charlottetown, or any other city in eastern Canada.

Statistically, Newfoundlanders are poor, with the highest unemploy-ment rate of any Canadian province. In reality, they are rich, and realize the fact. They have a greater cultural wealth, a greater ability to stretch resources into material comfort, a greater sense of optimism and sheer buoyancy, than any other people in Canada. They know for sure that they'll come out on top, because they always have, in spite of everything.

HAROLD HORWOOD

FALSE DAWN AT L'ANSE AUX MEADOWS—The European discovery of America may have begun here on the northern tip of Newfoundland—if it didn't begin even earlier elsewhere on the island. Around A.D. 1005 Norse settlers led by Thorfinn Karlsefni founded a colony that lasted only two or three years before conflicts with native peoples—Indians and Inuit—forced a retreat to Greenland and Iceland. Thorfinn's colonists wasted much time looking for "Vinland," reported earlier by Leif the Lucky, son of Eric the Red. But the site of their Norse farm complex (discovered here by the Norwegian explorer Helge Ingstad in 1960) was subsequently occupied by other Norse settlers, for a total of some twenty years, early in the eleventh century, before the Norse finally abandoned their attempt to colonize the new land. Later expeditions to "Markland" for timber probably went no farther than Labrador. The amateur historian W. A. Munn of St. John's suggested in 1929 that the Norse sagas pointed to this region. His book was used by Jorgen Meldgaard of Denmark for an archaeological search in 1959. In 1960 Ingstad was led directly to the site by Meldgaard's assistants who had decided, over the winter, that the mounds at L'Anse aux Meadows must be the buried ruins that the Europeans were looking for. Archaeologists quickly authenticated the find as a small farm complex similar to those in western Greenland, and dated it to approximately A.D. 1000.

CAPE FREELS FISHERMEN LAUNCHING BOAT—This is the way it started, almost five hundred years ago, with fishermen rolling their boats into the water. A Norse colony survived a short while in Newfoundland back in the eleventh century. Bristol merchants tried to found a colony as early as 1503. But the fishermen, interested only in the salt fish trade, were flocking to Newfoundland ports and setting up fishing premises on the island from the first years of the sixteenth century. The colonies came and went. Most of them failed. But the fishery went on without a break. Newfoundland fish was a common item of trade in Europe by 1508, and by the time of Sir Richard Whitbourne, one hundred years later, some ten thousand people were producing more than twenty million pounds of dried fish annually. English, Portuguese, French, and Spanish merchants shared the Newfoundland fishery, but only the English dried their fish ashore, salting it only lightly because they had to buy salt in foreign markets. This quickly led to a permanent occupation, to the kind of "outport" that still exists today, with salt stores, fish sheds, drying platforms, and a winter boat-building industry. By the time the first official colony was founded under royal patent in 1610, most of the east coast harbours were already occupied by permanent fishing establishments. After four-and-a-half centuries, the methods of the fishery have changed, but only in minor ways—millions of pounds of codfish are still landed from small boats by "shore" fishermen, as in Whitbourne's time.

L'ANSE AUX MEADOWS RESTORATION (left)—Rebuilt on the foundations excavated by Ingstad and Canadian archaeologists working with him, the Norse settlement at the Strait of Belle Isle now looks somewhat as it must have looked in the days when Thorfinn and his colonists from Iceland and Greenland first established their colony. This site was not the "landfall of Leif the Lucky." It bears no resemblance to Leif's landfall as described in the Norse sagas. The Icelanders, and all subsequent explorers, failed to find the temporary huts in which Leif's expedition spent their single winter. Leif's Vinland, the harbour called "Hop," and other possible Norse sites, remain to be discovered. At present this is the oldest known European settlement in North America. By the time English fishermen and Basque whalers began visiting Iceland and Greenland in the fifteenth century, the colony that Icelanders and Greenlanders had founded in Newfoundland four hundred years earlier had almost been forgotten. It is uncertain whether the Norse discovery and settlement had any real effect on the later discovery of the Grand Bank fisheries and of the island of Newfoundland itself. Though there is some meadow land at this site, the name L'Anse aux Meadows has nothing to do with grass. It is a corruption of the French *l'anse aux medeuses*—the cove of jellyfish.

Portuguese ships, st. john's—The Portuguese have fished in Newfoundland throughout the entire recorded history of the island. They claim to have discovered it before John Cabot reached the "New Founde Island" in 1497, and there is some evidence that Joao Vas Corte Real may have reached the "Island of Stockfish" in 1472. In any case they were fishing the Banks and frequenting St. John's harbour as early as 1506, two years before the first French ships arrived. Indeed, three Portuguese merchants from the Azores were included with three English merchants from Bristol in a "patent" issued by Henry VII in 1501, giving them rights in the New Founde Island. In that same year the King issued a second patent to another group of merchants, including two Portuguese, granting them a monopoly of the Newfoundland trade for a period of forty years. Portugal was only one of the early "discoverers" of Newfoundland, but more than any other nation has maintained friendly relations with the island and its people over more than four centuries. The Portuguese fleet fishing the western Atlantic and the Greenland Sea makes regular visits to St. John's, and in autumn during the hurricane season often takes shelter in the same port. From this harbour in 1527 John Rut, an explorer sent out to seek a Northwest Passage by King Henry VIII, sent the King a letter dated the third day of August, explaining that he had been stopped by ice off Labrador, and had spent the summer fishing. On arriving at St. John's he found eleven ships from Normandy, one from Brittany, and two from Portugal, but at that time the Portuguese were fishing mostly to the south, in Placentia Bay, while the Basques fished farther north, especially in the Strait of Belle Isle and on southern Labrador.

Basque fisherman, placentia (right)—The Basques also had a very early presence in Newfoundland, both as fishermen, working under the French, and as whalers, making "trayne oil." The Basques were a subject nation, their provinces divided between France and Spain. They were great seafarers, whalers, and ironworkers, and pursued the whaling trade as far as Greenland in the fifteenth century. It has not been established whether they reached Labrador before Cabot, but a major Basque whaling station dating from the early sixteenth century has recently been explored by marine archaeologists in southern Labrador. Making trayne oil from whales or seals to light the lamps of Europe was then a major industry. Some idea of the size of the operation may be gathered from the records of 1577 when a number of Basque ships were frozen into harbour in the Strait of Belle Isle, forcing the men to overwinter there. Though they must have had limitless supplies of fish and oil, they nevertheless died like flies, probably from scurvy. When the fleet reached home the next year five hundred and forty of its men were dead. Richard Whitbourne, the major chronicler of sixteenth-century Newfoundland, made his first voyage to the Strait of Belle Isle as mate of a ship in 1579. Making trayne oil was the object of the voyage, but the captain grew faint-hearted in the presence of the Basque whalers, and sailed off southward to spend the summer fishing in more familiar waters.

CLOSE TO THIS COMMANDING AND
HISTORIC SPOT SIR HUMPHREY GILBERT
LANDED ON THE 5TH DAY OF AUGUST 1583
AND IN TAKING POSSESSION OF THIS
NEW FOUND LAND IN THE NAME OF HIS
SOVEREIGN QUEEN ELIZABETH THEREBY
FOUNDED BRITAIN'S OVERSEAS EMPIRE

HUMPHREY GILBERT PLAQUE, ST. JOHN'S—This city that describes itself as the oldest in North America (true only if you exclude the cities of Mexico) was already the capital of the New World fisheries when Sir Humphrey Gilbert, a court favourite of Queen Elizabeth I, landed at this spot, raised the Cross of St. George, and proclaimed the rule of English law in Newfoundland. The date: August 3, 1583. "We made ready our fights and prepared to enter the harbour, any resistance to the contrary notwithstanding, there being within of all nations to the number of 36 sail." The English merchants, who controlled the harbour, at first opposed Gilbert's entry, but "being shown our commission, were all satisfied." Learning that he was sent by the Queen, they ordered a vice-regal welcome and "caused forthwith to be discharged all the great ordinance of their fleet." It was a gesture only. Gilbert departed after seventeen days in St. John's, mostly devoted to feasting and other entertainments, and was lost with all hands in his ship on the return voyage to England. St. John's then returned to the rule of the fishing admirals—the first captain of an English ship to enter a port in the spring became "admiral" for the rest of the year. These admirals held court and dispensed some form of amateur justice, mainly settling disputes over fishing premises—"rooms" as they were called. Gilbert, just the same, had founded on that August day in 1583 what was later to be called the British Empire, with Newfoundland as the oldest colony.

Row houses, st. john's—Parts of the old city, even now, look more like Europe than North America. In Gilbert's time there were two main streets (probably mere cart tracks) known as the Upper Path and the Lower Path. They are now Water Street and Duckworth-New Gower Street, still the commercial centre of the province of Newfoundland, though much of the city's activity, including the seat of government, has been moved away from the waterfront to what were then the berry barrens and hunting grounds on the high land to the north. A house suitable for an English courtier was provided by the merchants for Gil-

bert's use, but we have only a few rough sketches to suggest what St. John's looked like during its first two-and-a-half centuries. Repeated fires have wiped out all the early buildings. Just a few structures of stone and masonry survived the holocausts of the nineteenth century. But the style still echoes an earlier era. St. John's was never an official "colony," was never "founded" by English or any other immigrants. It was simply there, firmly established by trade and commerce, long before the first colonies were founded, either by French or English, in any part of what is now Canada.

THE MURRAY PREMISES, ST. JOHN'S—This beautifully preserved merchant house, built on a waterfront site that has been occupied since the sixteenth century, illustrates the *raison d'être* of the city of St. John's to perfection. The Newfoundland capital was originally, and always has remained, a merchants' town, with international traders striking bargains on its docks. Cargoes of fish and trayne oil were bought and sold on this spot, and shipped to all the major ports of Europe, both before and after the first beaver skins were traded at Port Royal and Quebec. Elizabeth issued licences to merchants to trade Newfoundland fish to any port in the world, in French as well as English carriers. The oldest surviving insurance policies issued in England are for cargoes of Newfoundland fish and trayne oil. The

trayne oil was not made by English fishing crews, at this early period, but was bartered for fish and for English woolens on the St. John's waterfront, being purchased from Basque whalers and shipped out in "hogsheads"—oversized barrels with a capacity of 63 imperial gallons. Fish was also shipped in hogsheads, but more often in bulk, and curiously enough was sold in the sixteenth century not by weight, but by the "cod's tail." A typical bill of lading for the period refers to 130,000 dry fish, and indeed they were sold on European markets by the dozen, like eggs. Gradually the "quintal"—112 pounds of dry fish—replaced this system and remained standard until the second half of the twentieth century.

THE BATTERY *(right)*— This part of St. John's, a captive "outport" inside the city, has changed hardly at all since its life began with the first shore-based fishermen. The name "Battery" refers to the fact that guns were emplaced here and at several other points on the hills overlooking The Narrows to defend the harbour of St. John's from attacks by pirates, privateers, and the warships of hostile nations. The oldest recorded defence of St. John's was in 1673, when Captain Christopher Martin, the fishing admiral for that year, took guns from the fishing ships, placed them in earthworks at The Battery, and beat off an attack by four Dutch privateers under the command of Captain Jacob Everson, but Martin mentions in his report that he had

defended the harbour with his own guns and ammunition on two previous occasions, in 1665 and 1667. Martin was Admiral or Vice-admiral of St. John's for seventeen years. The hijacking of cargoes in Newfoundland waters was so common that it was hardly even called by its proper name of "piracy." Captains sailing under both Sir Walter Raleigh and Sir Humphrey Gilbert seized cargoes of French fish by force, and even in at least one instance robbed French sailors of their clothing, at a time when England and France were not at war. The French regularly sued for damages, but had great difficulty in collecting any compensation. Whitbourne, one of Martin's predecessors at St. John's, referred to such part-time pirates as "erring captains."

Hibbs cove *(right)*— The name is a modern gloss of the traditional name Hibbs's Hole, a productive fishing station, "across the tickle" from Cupids, where John Guy of the London and Bristol Company founded his colony in 1610. The choice of Cupids, a harbourless cove without promising waterfront for a fishing industry, has sometimes puzzled historians, but is easily understood when it is realized that every good harbour, such as this, was already occupied by fishermen before Guy and his colonists arrived. Guy's colony was to act as a form of support for the fishing industry by establishing secondary industries, including farming and the milling of grain—it was, in fact, the first attempt at "economic development" in Newfoundland, a theme that has occupied practically every government from Guy's time to the present. The colony did some farming, built a grist mill on the river running into this arm of Conception Bay, and established a cooperage for making barrels and drums, and such small enterprises as blacksmith sheds and charcoal manufacture. Except for the grist mill, however, these were all enterprises that the fishermen were carrying on before the colonists arrived. There was even a little gardening being done, as noted by the colonists' clerk, who saw men from nearby settlements hauling loads of caplin from the beaches to manure their ground. The colony languished, but the surrounding fishing settlements flourished. Newfoundland was no place for grain fields, but for "cod's heads and cabbage patches" it just couldn't be beat.

Peter easton plaque—By 1610 piracy in Newfoundland was no longer the work of mere amateurs, but had become big business. From 1610 to 1614—the years bracketing the founding of the Cupids colony—the pirate admiral Captain Peter Easton made his principal base in Newfoundland. He built a fort at Harbour Grace, took the supplies of the Cupids colonists under his protection (to defend them from robbers or pirates of other nations), and raided the shipping and the shore stations of all nations from Newfoundland to the Caribbean. He crowned his career by capturing the Spanish plate fleet at the Azores in 1614, and then retired to the French Riviera, where he "lived rich." His principal form of piracy in the island of Newfoundland was the recruiting of some five hundred fishermen to man his ten pirate ships. The English merchants, infuriated by Easton, persuaded the government to send out a squadron of warships to bring him to justice, but the squadron, commanded by Henry Mainwaring, turned pirate in turn, and took command of Easton's fort at Harbour Grace after Easton had moved to Ferryland, south of St. John's. Mainwaring also recruited Newfoundland fishermen for his crews, but was careful to avoid attacking English shipping. He had "eight sail of strong ships, well armed" while in Newfoundland. After defeating a Spanish naval squadron fitted out especially to do battle with him, he was invited home to England, knighted, and elected to Parliament, finally becoming Vice-admiral and commander of the British fleet.

PETER EASTON

PETER EASTON "THE PIRATE ADMIRAL" FORTIFIED THIS SITE IN 1610 AND MADE NEWFOUNDLAND HIS BASE UNTIL 1614. HE DEFEATED A FRENCH SQUADRON AT HARBOUR GRACE IN 1611, RECRUITED 5,000 FISHERMEN FROM THIS COLONY INTO HIS CREWS, AND RAIDED FOREIGN SHIPPING AS FAR AS THE CARIBBEAN. IN 1614 HE INTERCEPTED THE SPANISH PLATE FLEET AT THE AZORES, CAPTURED THREE TREASURE SHIPS, AND DIVIDED AN IMMENSE FORTUNE AMONG HIS CREWS. HE WAS TWICE PARDONED AND INVITED HOME BY JAMES I, BUT RETIRED INSTEAD TO SOUTHERN FRANCE WHERE HE BECAME MARQUIS OF SAVOY AND LIVED IN GREAT SPLENDOR.

ERECTED BY THEIR FRIENDS IN MEMORY OF
JEROME C.º & PAMELA E. BARTER LEE
& FIRST CURATOR CONCEPTION BAY MUSEUM 1976

BEOTHUK BONE PENDANTS—Establishing trade with the native Indians was another object of the London and Bristol Company. John Guy sailed into Trinity Bay where the fishermen reported that bands of Beothuks or Red Indians as they were called (because they painted themselves with red ochre) often came down to the coast in summer. Guy's ship was not well equipped for trading, but he did meet a small band of Beothuks, who welcomed him with singing, dancing, and an eagerness to exchange presents that showed they were no strangers to Europeans. They made an agreement to meet at the same place for far more extensive trading the following summer. But Guy went home to England and did not return. Next year an English fishing ship anchored off the same beach where Guy had traded

with the Indians. Canoe-loads of Beothuks promptly headed for the ship, shouting a welcome, while others danced and sang on shore. The fishermen interpreted this as a war dance and the canoe flotilla as an attack. They opened fire with their ship's guns, sending the Indians fleeing into the woods. There are few recorded instances of peaceful contact between the Beothuks and the English settlers after this incident. The Beothuks stole fishing gear from the settlers' stages, and the settlers took to raiding Beothuk camps and stealing their furs. In time these raids against Indian camps developed into genocidal attacks in which every Indian that came within range of the settlers' guns were killed.

BEOTHUK CHILD'S SHOES *(right)*— Such pathetic relics as these were all that remained of the Beothuk Indians even early in the nineteenth century. They never took up the use of firearms, and apparently had no tradition of warfare. An insular people who had been in Newfoundland for many centuries, they had little contact with other Indian tribes, and hence no tradition of organizing war parties. They were quite unequal to any kind of struggle with the settlers, who had muskets, powder, balls, and swan shot, and who took up hunting Indians as a sport. This form of murder was not even recognized as a crime until the administration of Governor Sir Hugh Palliser (1764–1768), who failed to save the Beothuks but managed to save the Inuit of Labrador from a similar fate. Even in Palliser's time, and after,

Beothuks were killed with impunity. Threats of prosecution had no effect, and though one or two murders were investigated, no one in Newfoundland was ever actually punished for killing an Indian. Towards the end the government offered a reward of fifty pounds sterling to anyone who would bring a captive Beothuk to St. John's, on the hope that peaceful trade could be established through such a captive. But the result was that Beothuk men were slaughtered in an effort to kidnap their women and claim the reward. The last such captive, taken by a family of Indian-killers named Payton at Twillingate, died at St. John's in 1829. No trace was found of twelve others, known to be still loose in the woods when she surrendered to the White men.

BALTIMORE COAT OF ARMS, FERRYLAND—Sometimes called "the first English capital" of Newfoundland, Ferryland was the seat of the first English governor to be given at least nominal jurisdiction over the whole island. That was in 1637, the year Newfoundland was granted its coat of arms by King Charles I. Even before that time it had been the centre of another colonizing enterprise by Sir George Calvert, Lord Baltimore, who later colonized Maryland. Baltimore's agents, with colonists, were at Ferryland on September 5, 1621, but the royal patent for the colony was not issued until April 7, 1623, and Baltimore himself did not arrive until 1627. Among schemes just as impractical as the growing of wheat and rye by Guy's colonists was the commercial production of wine by Baltimore's. Samples were ordered sent to England, with unrecorded results. The wine might possibly have been made from wild grapes (recorded as growing at Ferryland in the seventeenth century) but more likely from the abundant blueberries that were used, much later, to produce commercial wine in Nova Scotia, and which have provided "country wine" time out of mind in Newfoundland. Baltimore built a great stone house at Ferryland, but soon discovered that the winter climate there did not suit him, and abandoned his colony to agents. The house was later occupied by Sir David Kirke, the first governor with island-wide jurisdiction, but Kirke was sued by Baltimore's agents, and died in jail in England before the dispute came to trial.

FERRYLAND—David Kirke was the eldest of five brothers who held privateering commissions from the English government. Their fleet of five ships blockaded the St. Lawrence River in 1628, and captured the large French supply fleet sent out to reinforce the Quebec colony. The following year the fleet captured Quebec, taking Champlain prisoner. Three years later, the English agreed by treaty to return Quebec to France, though the Kirkes were not actually dislodged from Quebec until 1533. David was knighted and given the governorship of Newfoundland by King Charles I, but was accused by the colonizing company of using his position to enrich himself, by trading, opening taverns, and forcibly taking over properties held by others. John Downing replaced him as head of the colonizing company, but Kirke remained at Ferryland, apparently in royal favour and in nominal authority, even though he was no longer in charge of colonizing efforts. He was still at Ferryland in 1649, when Charles I had lost his throne and was about to lose his head to the Commonwealth under Cromwell. Kirke offered the King asylum in Newfoundland, which he was prepared to defend against Cromwell's ships, but Charles chose to remain in England and face execution, thereby saving the English monarchy, even while losing his own life. Though Sir David Kirke returned to England to answer charges by Baltimore's supporters, his family remained as planters at Ferryland, and three families of Kirkes were still there, employing fourteen fishing boats and sixty-six fishermen, when the Dutch attacked Newfoundland in 1663.

FISH DRYING ON FLAKE—In a thousand outports for some three hundred years this was the signature of summer. Methods of catching fish changed at least a little. Baited hand lines were gradually replaced by cod seines, which, however, had the disadvantage of killing the fish, which then became soft before it could be cured, producing an inferior product. The seines eventually gave way to cod traps, box-shaped nets that impounded the fish but did not kill them. Cod traps produced massive amounts of live fish, and are still one of the best methods of fishing during the height of the summer runs when a single trap will often yield many thousands of pounds of fish a day. The baited hand lines were replaced by long-lines, with many baited

hooks spun out of a tub by a moving boat. Lures called "jiggers" were developed and improved. But once the fish was landed, it was handled by the same traditional method that the first bye-boatmen had brought with them from the south of England. It was not until the 1940s that fresh frozen fish began to replace salt dried fish as the major Newfoundland food export, and it was not until the 1950s that salt fish began to be processed in artificial drying plants, rather than on flakes in the sun. Then the square miles of fish flakes that had been the trademark of the outports began to disappear. A few fish processors still use flakes to dry at least part of the catch, for no artificial dryer yet invented has been able to match the flavour of natural sun-cured fish.

FISH FLAKE, BADGER'S QUAY(left)— By the mid-seventeenth century, with the rise of the bye-boatmen, the Newfoundland cod fishery had settled into the form it would keep for the next three centuries. Bye-boatmen were men who fished from shore stations, operating their own small boats, not attached to a fishing ship, or to a major "plantation" as the big fishing premises were called. Bye-boatmen were what we would now call shore fishermen. They built fish stores, where they cleaned and stored their fish, and fish flakes on which to cure it, almost always within a short walk of their houses. As they became dominant in the cod fishery, they gradually ringed Newfoundland with fish flakes—flimsy-looking platforms like this one, built of "starrigans" and

small poles from the adjoining forest, topped with "longers" and with boughs of spruce or fir. On such structures the fish, after splitting, cleaning, and salting, were spread to dry in the sun, collected into small piles, and covered when rain threatened or the sun grew dangerously hot. Carefully carried on, and with some co-operation from the weather, this process produced a premium grade of fish that fetched the highest prices in world markets, not only in such countries as Italy and Brazil that produced no salt fish of their own, but even in Spain and Portugal, where large fisheries carried on from ships yielded massive catches that never matched the quality of Newfoundland Shore Cure.

GARDEN PATCH, STARRIGAN FENCE—Like the fishery, home economy in Newfoundland changed little in three hundred years. The caplin-fertilized vegetable plots that Guy's colonists saw in nearby outports remained vital to the outport people, who fed themselves from three sources: the sea, the woods, and their own back yards. Starrigans, dry saplings cut from the woods, were as important as the few square rods of spaded soil, for in Newfoundland such animals as sheep, goats, horses, and cows were never fenced in; they roamed at large, and had to be fenced out. Goats in particular were great fence-breakers, able to worm their way through almost any small gap, and were often fitted with wooden yokes to make their exits and entrances more difficult. Agriculture remained a dream of governments and colonizing companies, but contributed little to the merchant economy. The stony or boggy soil of Newfoundland was fit only for determined home gardeners, but most fishing families managed to make it grow enough cabbages, turnips, and potatoes to feed themselves. A few progressive gardeners also grew all the carrots and beets they needed. Parsnips flourished so well that they became a favourite vegetable with thousands of outport people. Reliance on the back-yard vegetable patch didn't begin to decline until Newfoundland entered Confederation with Canada, and money became plentiful.

Trinity—Nobody knows where the first permanent settlers made their homes and built their fish stores in Newfoundland, but Trinity has a very ancient claim. This lovely village, with perhaps the most intimate mixture of land and sea in Canada, received what may have been its first shipload of settlers in 1558 when Captain Robert Ward landed there in the brig *Hawke*, with ten families, totalling forty-three people. Three years later the *Osprey*, also of Plymouth, landed thirteen families, totalling forty-eight. In 1579 Richard Whitbourne bought fish and poultry from the inhabitants. In 1616 the Wards of Plymouth opened a branch of their merchant house at Trinity and it remained a trading centre for three centuries, with fishing, farming, and shipbuilding. It was here that Whitbourne held the first Vice-admiralty Court ever convened outside the Realm of England, on Trinity Sunday (June 4), 1615. One hundred and seventy fishing masters attended the court. In the year General Wolfe sailed against Quebec, Trinity had 1,369 inhabitants. By the end of the eighteenth century there was a shipyard in each of its three arms, building one of every four ships launched in Newfoundland. In the 1980s there were still three shipyards in the same locations. Tourists had replaced fish as a major industry, and Trinity had its professional whale watcher, Peter Beamish, with his whale museum perched on a headland from which it is possible to see schools of great whales any day in summer.

LESTER-GARLAND STORE, TRINITY (right)—This was the main store of the Lester-Garland commercial empire. Restored to the way it appeared in 1820, it is being restocked as a museum with furnishings and chattels of the period. It stands beside the ruins of the Garland House, an old mansion that would more properly be called the Lester House, since it was built by the merchant Benjamin Lester in 1750, and was used as a dwelling-house by his descendants until 1950. The house was inherited from Benjamin Lester by his son-in-law, George Garland Sr., who expanded the Lester business into northern Newfoundland and Labrador. Garland became vastly wealthy, and was the mayor of Pool in England, as well as a Member of Parliament there. His son, John Bingley Garland, moved to Trinity, and later to St. John's, upon being elected to the first House of Assembly, of which he became first Speaker. Like St. Paul's Church, the Lester House passed through several restorations, and appears to have been virtually rebuilt by the Garland family early in the nineteenth century. Built of English brick, with a roof of English slate, it was allowed to collapse after 1950. Workmen began tearing it down, until frantic calls from the historic sites commission stopped the destruction. No one could find the money for its restoration, however. An estimate for restoring it in 1980 ran to more than $2-million.

ST. PAUL'S ANGLICAN CHURCH—Built originally in 1730, and three times restored, this is perhaps the loveliest small church in Newfoundland. It is filled with graceful wooden arches. The rising sun illuminates a stained-glass crucifix over the altar. The setting sun shines through opulent reds and blues of a great transfiguration scene in stained glass standing above the baptismal font. It has the kind of modest magnificence that is truly typical of Trinity, as proud and dignified as it is old. The stones in the churchyard date from 1736. It is surrounded by white colonial houses, some of them impressively large, most of them ringed with lilacs and peonies planted one or two centuries ago, reminding the visitor of the old settlements in New England. Nearby is a monument to Dr. John Clinch, a friend of Dr. William Jenner, the discoverer of the smallpox vaccine. Clinch was stationed at Trinity as an Anglican priest, where he performed the first smallpox vaccinations in the western hemisphere. It was the beginning of the world-wide extermination of one of the most dreaded and lethal of all human diseases.

PRINCESS SHEILA—This old gravestone at Carbonear no longer has any legible inscription, but the family that treasures it insists that it was cut for Princess Sheila "Nagira," the ancestor of a large Newfoundland family. Tradition says she was the daughter of the Celtic King of Connaught. This, according to Irish history, would make her an O'Connor, descendant of a family that had once been High Kings of Ireland, and would explain why she was sent out of Ireland in the last days of the reign of Elizabeth I, when the O'Connors were fighting on *both sides* of Elizabeth's last Irish war. Destined for a convent in France, Princess Sheila was captured by privateers, liberated by an English warship, and arrived in Newfoundland with the fishing convoy,

as wife of a young lieutenant, Gilbert Pike. The lieutenant settled with her at Mosquito (now called Bristol's Hope), a fishing cove between Carbonear and Harbour Grace. If the Pikes actually arrived on the convoy in question, there is no doubt about its date: 1602. Even so, they may not have been the first land-takers at Mosquito. According to the page of an old family Bible recorded in the Conception Bay Museum, the first might have been Robert Tossey:

Tossey's son of Dartmouth Town,
A mariner bold of great renown
Who crossed the sea in fifteen hundred and eighty-three
To settle down in Muscatown.

OUTPORT BEDROOM—The modest elegance of this austere room in the museum at Ferryland illustrates the life of the Newfoundland "planters" from the early days down to the end of the nineteenth century. Chairs such as this were manufactured by local craftsmen, following European models. They often imitated such classics as Sheridan, Chippendale, or the Queen Anne style. The dresser or "highboy" was also locally made. Everything else in the room—the pottery, the steel-and-brass bedstead, the sheets, the cloth for the "runner" on the dresser—would be imported from England. Needlework embroidery on runner and bedspread were always crafted by the mother of the family or an older daughter. The crucifix would not have been displayed in the seventeenth or eighteenth centuries, when the Roman Catholic religion was still proscribed in Newfoundland. Though no law against the practice of Catholicism was ever promulgated in the colony, the savage anti-Catholic laws of Ireland were held to apply. Anyone who "harboured a priest" was liable to have his house and fishing property torn down or burnt, and might also be fined, flogged, or banished. The penal restrictions were gradually relaxed around the year 1800, and by 1806, when the first public Catholic institutions were forming, freedom of religion was generally accepted, though riots based on religious intolerance might still occur.

NEWFOUNDLAND WATER DOGS—One of two distinct Newfoundland breeds of dogs, this animal is of obscure origin.
It was present from the earliest recorded times, but whether
it evolved among the Beothuk Indians or the early European settlers remains a question. The settlers brought "mas-
tiff dogs" from Europe, as Captain Whitbourne recorded, in
the sixteenth century, but at the same time the "wolves and
beasts of the country" intermingled with the immigrant
dogs, and settlers raiding Beothuk camps reported dogs in
their tents. Whatever its origin, the Newfoundland water
dog was the world's only dog with webbed feet. It became
the ancestor of the Labrador retriever, and all other breeds
of retriever, such as the Chesapeake Bay, that have webbed
feet. Another breed, the Newfoundland, developed near St.
John's, out of working dogs used to haul wood sleds.
Originally black and white and small-headed, this second
breed was converted by dog-fanciers into a huge, shaggy,
coal-black animal, with a substantial dash of St. Bernard in
its ancestry. Dogs, whether for retrieving birds or hauling
sleds, were almost as essential to pioneer Newfoundlanders
as they were to the Inuit people of Labrador. The breeds
were maintained by survival of the fittest, and became
exceptionally intelligent and sweet-tempered animals: there
is simply no such thing as a vicious Newfoundland dog of
either breed. The water dogs are short-coated, and great
swimmers.

NEWFOUNDLAND PONIES—The distinctive little working horse of Newfoundland evolved from animals brought to the island by fishermen in pre-colonial times. They were already working in the fishing settlements when the Cupids Colony was founded in 1610. They have maintained their distinctive characteristics ever since: exceptional hardiness, sure-footedness, and an ability to live off the roughest kind of wild pasture. Used for ploughing and cultivating, and for hauling firewood, and fish guts and caplin for fertilizer, they demanded little from their owners beyond a few bales of winter hay—cut from cultivated ground or wild marsh lands. Traditionally, they ran loose in small herds throughout the summer, and were rounded up and identified by their owners, often from considerable distances, in autumn, when they were harnessed and put back to work hauling firewood, saw logs, or "longers" for fences and next year's fishing stages. Dogs and horses were not the only distinct breeds of animals bred by the colonists. They also evolved their own races of sheep and goats—both of them, like the horses, hardier and better able to live off the country than any imported breed. All these native animals have declined greatly in number during recent decades, but none of the native breeds appears in immediate danger of extinction. All have dominant characteristics and tend to "breed true" despite much crossing.

PLACENTIA—Sometimes called the "French capital" of Newfoundland, Placentia was first a Portuguese fishing station, and later a centre for the great French fishery, where French and Basque fleets arrived each year to be apportioned fishing rooms not only in the immediate vicinity of the harbour, but also on all the coasts of Newfoundland where fishing and whaling were pursued under French jurisdiction. Two rivers meet in Placentia harbour, and on one of them—Northeast River—the French created a large shipbuilding industry. Placentia was ruled by a military governor, under the Comte de Frontenac, governor of New France, and was used as the base for a series of raids, by

FRENCH OFFICER, 1696 (left)—In the year 1662 Newfoundland history took a sharp turn into one hundred years of warfare. After more than a century during which the English in Newfoundland went unchallenged except for occasional raids by pirates and privateers, the French built a great fort at Placentia, as part of a chain of fortifications stretching through St. Pierre and Cape Breton into the Gulf of St. Lawrence and on to Quebec City. Soon they were marching back and forth across the island, burning the fishing settlements, capturing the small forts built by the English, and shipping the English colonists (most of whom had been born in Newfoundland) "back to England" in an operation very similar to the famous expulsion of the

land and by sea, against the English settlements. An English fleet, sent to capture the fort, retreated without pressing the siege. In fact, throughout its history first as a French and later as an English fortress, Placentia was never successfully attacked, except by pirates, who managed to land and loot a good portion of the town, as they did at so many other places along the Atlantic seaboard. From Placentia Basque privateers sailed under French letters of marque to attack Ferryland, St. John's, and smaller English settlements. From here, too, the French launched their raids of extermination overland to St. John's, and into Conception and Trinity bays.

Acadians from Nova Scotia some sixty years later. None of the raids was ever completely successful. A few outposts of the English-speaking settlers held out. Some of the fishing families escaped to the woods, and returned to rebuild a few weeks later, only to be raided and burnt out once again. The French simply had no troops to garrison the Newfoundland settlements, and consequently were wholly unable to hold the colony against determined resistance by the colonists. the colonists. Their presence was limited to the forts, and to a chain of small fishing settlements along the south coast of Newfoundland, where English colonists did not penetrate until the Treaty of Utrecht brought a temporary end to the fighting in 1713.

BASQUE GRAVESTONE—John Svigaricipi, a Basque privateer sailing out of Placentia, became a great naval hero in the series of wars between the French and English in the later years of the seventeenth century. Svigaricipi captured hundreds of merchant vessels belonging to English or Newfoundland merchants and fishing masters, and even managed to capture some English warships, among them the 100-gun English ship of the line, *Princess*, a rare feat indeed for a privateer, leading to his being decorated by King Louis XIV of France. He was killed at sea, apparently in the French attempt to capture Ferryland in 1694. On that occasion the city was successfully defended by the local fishing masters, who took guns from their ships, emplaced them on Isle au Bois, and fought off the French squadron. Svigaricipi was buried at Placentia in the old churchyard first used by the Portuguese, and subsequently by the French, who rebuilt on the foundation of an earlier Portuguese church. His stone was preserved, after the English conquest, in the Church of England church, and was finally moved to the Interpretation Centre for Placentia, after the French forts were excavated on Castle Hill; some of the artefacts recovered were placed in the newly built Interpretation Centre, together with maps and pictures illustrating the history of the town.

FRENCH ARTILLERYMAN(right)— The French were better armed and far better at fortifications than the English. Technology and skill were pitted against numbers, for New France was always hopelessly outnumbered by the English colonies. When Pierre Le Moyne D'Iberville, with his brother and other skilful raiders, began his campaign against the English settlements in 1682, he was attacking an enemy that outnumbered him at least ten to one. His campaign against the Hudson Bay posts established his reputation, and he was in charge of the campaign against Newfoundland in 1694, when English fishermen manning improvised forts defeated French naval attacks on Ferryland and St. John's. D'Iberville then proposed to take the English settlements in the rear, by a march overland from Placentia—a kind of warfare that had not yet been attempted in Newfoundland. Nine privateers, two corvettes, and two fireships also sailed against St. John's. The naval attack failed completely, like others before it, but D'Iberville with his Canadian militiamen and Indian "braves" carried everything before him. Ferryland, Bay Bulls, St. John's, all fell in turn. The dead were scalped, and the scalps presented to Frontenac in Quebec. The settlements were burned. D'Iberville met no serious resistance until he reached Carbonear.

CARBONEAR ISLAND—St. John's was burned three times in French raids, and three times rebuilt. The settlements around Conception and Trinity bays went the same way. But the first D'Iberville raid was not a complete success. The great guerrilla fighter lingered at St. John's long enough to give the fishermen of Carbonear ample warning of what was in store for them. They collected all the guns they could find, with stores of powder and shot from their ships, and fortified Carbonear Island. Two French assaults by boat were defeated, and the Carbonear settlers withstood a siege until the French retreated to Placentia in the spring of 1697. Later that year, two regiments were sent out from England, and the fort at St. John's was rebuilt. For a time, the "English Shore" between Cape Race and Cape Bonavista was secure from attack. That year a temporary peace was concluded between the European powers, and the fighting in Newfoundland ceased for five years. The settlers rebuilt their houses and fishing stages. The ships from the English West Country returned, and were joined by other fishing crews from New England in an enterprise that employed some twenty thousand men each summer. The Newfoundland fishery was now one of England's largest industries, the greatest single overseas enterprise, and the very cradle and nursery of English sea power. It was to become a crucial factor in the final war for Canada.

CAPE BONAVISTA—Such settlements as Bonavista and Trinity, which lay to the north and west of D'Iberville's march, escaped the first great French raid. When the war was resumed in 1702, the French again attacked all the English settlements, and sent a naval force to destroy Bonavista. They were met, in 1704, by a well-organized defence under Captain Michael Gill, a New England fishing master. The 144 French Canadians, in two sloops and two boats, attacked the harbour on August 18 at two o'clock in the morning. Using two captured ships, the French engaged Gill's 14-gun ship in a naval battle that lasted six hours. They twice attempted to destroy him with fireships, but Gill managed to tow the fireships out of danger "labouring furiously in the fire." With the coming of full daylight, all the inhabitants appeared on the shore under arms, and the French made their escape, releasing in a boat the prisoners they had taken from the two captured ships. Gill had saved Bonavista by force of arms. The next year a Quaker fishing admiral, George Skiffington, saved it again by negotiation and payment of a ransom. Both Gill and Skiffington remained in Newfoundland and founded important families. The Skiffingtons became planters in Bonavista Bay, the Gills merchants and traders at St. John's and later in northern Newfoundland. With the Treaty of Utrecht (1713) peace returned for a time, and Placentia passed permanently into English hands.

BONNE BAY—With the Treaty of Utrecht the whole of Newfoundland became British territory, but the French retained the right to fish along the northern and western coasts, and to build temporary stations for curing fish on land. This was the origin of the "French Shore" as it came to be called. The exact boundaries of the French Shore varied under treaty, but most or all of the west coast of Newfoundland was included. Though from the English point of view this did not interfere with sovereignty, or the rights of settlement, the French interpreted the treaty another way—that any interference with their fishery (by building houses on the shore, for example) was illegal. So peaceable settlement on Newfoundland's highly attractive west coast was hampered and retarded for almost two centuries. Settlers' houses might be burned, their fish confiscated. The French patrolled the coast with armed ships each year. The English rarely put in an appearance. Even during periods of peace, therefore, a substantial part of Newfoundland remained effectively in French hands, though nominally under British rule. One of the relics of this period is a small French-speaking population still resident in western Newfoundland. The French Shore question was not settled until 1904, when France gave up her rights in Newfoundland in exchange for rights in Africa.

FORT AT QUIDI VIDI—The last battle for French Canada began here. After the loss of Quebec, the French countered by capturing St. John's, and attacking Ferryland and Placentia, reasoning that if they could hold Newfoundland until the war ended, the English would be willing to restore Quebec to French rule in exchange for Newfoundland. It was a very reasonable assumption, for the English had enormous financial interests in Newfoundland, and none whatever in Canada. The French failed, however, in their attacks on Ferryland and Placentia. They garrisoned St. John's with troops, stationed a strong flotilla in the harbour, and rebuilt and strengthened the forts both in the town and on Signal Hill, overlooking the harbour. The recapture of St. John's in 1762, three years after the fall of Quebec, became a crucial matter of British policy. Colonel William Amherst was brought from New York to take command of the counter-invasion. He had excellent troops under his command—Swiss and German mercenaries, and companies of three Scottish regiments from Cape Breton. Amherst's plan for the recapture of St. John's was faultless and economical. He landed at Torbay against virtually no resistance from the French, marched to Quidi Vidi, and captured the village in a brief battle with little loss of life on either side. He was now established in Newfoundland, but the real task of taking nearby St. John's, with its strong fortifications, remained. The date of the battle of Quidi Vidi was September 13, 1762.

ROYAL NFLD. REGIMENT, TATTOO ON SIGNAL HILL—Amherst now turned the guns of the fort on Quidi Vidi Heights against the fort on Signal Hill, and forced the French to retreat from the hill without a fight. By August 16 he had command of all the hills overlooking St. John's and the harbour, and the French position had become hopeless. The French fleet in St. John's harbour slipped quietly away in darkness and under cover of fog, and so escaped from the strong British naval squadron awaiting them offshore. Negotiations then began between Amherst, who had further strengthened his position on Signal Hill with guns and mortars, and the French commander, the Comte D'Haus-sonville, who still held a strong fort in St. John's itself. This fort, however, lay directly under Amherst's artillery, and if necessary could be slowly pounded into rubble. Amherst demanded that the French surrender without further battle, threatening that if he had to storm the fort he would "put every defender to the sword." This threat had its effect. D'Haussonville surrendered on terms: the French troops would keep their arms, and be embarked for France. So, in the most brilliant action of the entire war, Amherst recaptured St. John's on September 20, 1762, and the French Fleur de Lis came down over the last town in which it flew in what is now the nation of Canada.

MALLARD HOUSE, QUIDI VIDI (left)— This cottage, built in an English style of the seventeenth century, is believed to be the oldest house in English Canada, and has been occupied continuously by the Mallard family since it was built, following the French raids of the 1690s. At the Battle of Quidi Vidi in 1762 it was used as a dressing station for the English wounded. On the morning after the capture of Quidi Vidi Colonel Amherst opened the small channel into Quidi Vidi Gut, which the French had closed by sinking two shallops between the cliffs on either side. Amherst was then able to land stores and artillery, which he had been unable to bring overland from Torbay. The French still held two forts on hills, one above Quidi Vidi, the other on Signal Hill above St. John's. The first of these two forts, the one near Quidi Vidi, Amherst captured on September 15 with the loss of only four men and one officer, and eighteen wounded, by sending troops quietly up the hill in the fog before daybreak. They were not discovered by the sentries until they were established on ground overlooking the fort, and had it at their mercy. After a brief exchange of fire the French troops recognized the hopelessness of their situation, and surrendered. Amherst had now taken Quidi Vidi and the first French fort, and could land any quantity of supplies he needed, in safety. The capture of Signal Hill and St. John's remained to be accomplished.

GUNS AT BAY BULLS (*left*)—Once the wars with France were ended the British built strong fortifications in Newfoundland: Quidi Vidi, Signal Hill, Ferryland, Placentia, Trinity, Carbonear Island, were all fortified and garrisoned. Even Bay Bulls, where the French had landed to capture St. John's in 1762, was fortified with gun emplacements. As it turned out, Bay Bulls was the site of one last invasion. Though New France was irretrievably lost to the British, a French squadron was sent, during the Napoleonic Wars, to do whatever damage it could to the British cause in North America. The squadron landed troops at Bay Bulls and captured the small fort there without trouble. They planned to march from there to St. John's, but abandoned the plan, apparently because a prisoner gave them the false information that the Newfoundland capital was strongly defended by British regular troops. They re-embarked from Bay Bulls, and contented themselves with raiding merchant shipping and fishing stations as far northward as Labrador. Fears of a French attack on Quidi Vidi, or of an invasion of American troops during the War of Independence, proved groundless. Newfoundlanders had fought their last battle on their own soil—though they would fight many terrible battles elsewhere in future wars—and the guns that had been brought from Europe became mere decorations. Those at Bay Bulls became gateposts for the big Roman Catholic church.

SEAL HUNTERS—Ice drifting south with the Labrador Current arrives on the north and east coasts of Newfoundland each year in early spring. The ice-field, while still off Labrador, is used by the harp seal herd as a maternity ward and nursery for its pups. For about six weeks the young seals remain on the ice, drifting southward with it until they arrive somewhere off St. John's, when they take to the water and begin swimming northward to their summering grounds in the Canadian Arctic. A few stray seals come within sight of the land every year. Now and then a herd numbering tens or hundreds of thousands will be blown right into the northern bays. To early settlers these events were windfalls. Swarming over the ice on foot, they killed and hauled to land every seal they could reach. They gorged on fresh seal meat, salted it for themselves and their dogs, made boots and clothing from seal skins, sold the fat and surplus hides to the nearest merchant, who made the fat into trayne oil and shipped oil and hides to Europe. Soon the fishermen began hunting the seals in open boats, and by the end of the eighteenth century the merchants were fitting out ships to go hunting for the "main patch" off the north coast. By the time Napoleon was defeated, and the War of 1812 had been fought to a draw, sealing was a major industry, enriching the merchants and giving at least some of the fishermen a little spending money once a year.

ICE WITH BERG—Partly as a result of the seal hunting tradition, Newfoundlanders became experts at ice travel and ice navigation. Every Arctic explorer who knew anything about his business hired a Newfoundland sealing captain to "scun" his ship through the ice-fields, and trusted the captain to pick a crew of Newfoundlanders to sail with him into the ice. Frequently a Newfoundland sealing ship, strengthened internally for operation in ice, and sheathed in greenheart to prevent her planking from being cut through, would be chartered to sail north to Baffin Bay, Greenland, and the Canadian Arctic Islands. When the expeditions became stranded, as they regularly did, Newfoundland ships and sealing crews would be hired once more to go to the rescue. It is a remarkable fact that in dozens of such expeditions there was almost no loss of life. The Newfoundland sealing captains were able to take their ships into the most unlikely nooks and crannies of the high Arctic, and get them out again, with all their crews on board. One of them explained their success for the American press: "Compared to the seal fishery, a voyage to the Arctic is a mere picnic. When we're out after swiles we're dealing every day with worse conditions and greater danger than you ever meet along the coast of Greenland."

ICE *(right)*—This is what they had to face, every year, in small wooden ships, for the mere chance of a few dollars. They were signed on for no wages, but for a share of the catch *after expenses*. If they returned with few seals they got nothing. Fifty dollars was the sealer's share of a good paying voyage. The golden prospect of collecting $100 or even more from a "bumper trip to the ice" kept them going back, year after year, living in conditions hardly fit for dogs, eating hard tack washed down with black tea, ravenously consuming the first seal meat, risking death daily. Hundreds of ships went down, crushed in the ice, but when that happened the ice was usually so close-packed that the men could walk ashore. Much more dangerous was the risk of getting separated from the ship in a storm, stranded on drifting ice, freezing to death. It happened many times. More than a thousand Newfoundland men and boys lost their lives hunting seals. The harp seal herd dwindled, and the hood seals became rare, but new technology—first wooden steamships, then steel ice-breakers, then aircraft—kept the catches large. Some years more than half a million pelts arrived on the docks at Brigus, Harbour Grace, and St. John's, even though half the kill was usually lost at sea. A herd that may once have numbered ten million was reduced to about one-twentieth its original size.

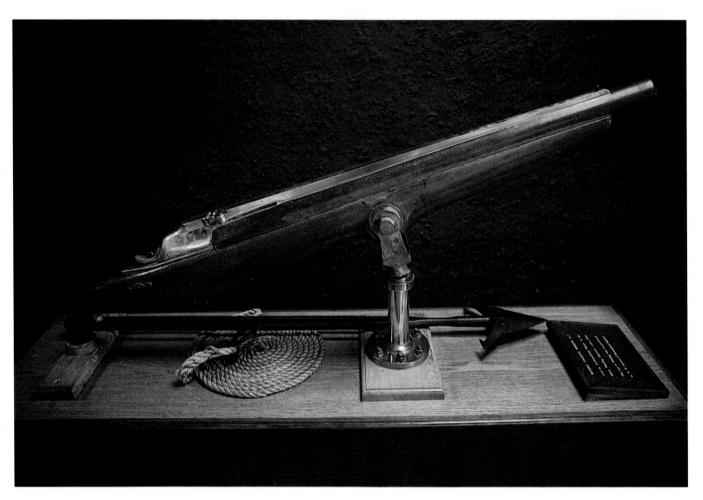

WHALING GUN AND HARPOON—Whale hunting goes back to pre-colonial times. The Dorset people of northern and western Newfoundland hunted small whales. The Beothuk Indians carved whales' tails on their tribal staves. The Basques had a great whaling industry in the Strait of Belle Isle at the same time that the early fishing crews were working out of St. John's. American whalers were working in the Strait before the War of Independence, but there was no whale hunt in English Newfoundland, except along the south coast, where crews of Jerseymen, working for merchants from the Channel Islands, hunted whales in open boats, and made trayne oil at small shore stations. As an organized industry, the whale hunt did not begin in English Newfoundland until late colonial times, long after the seal hunt was well established. Small whaling stations were then opened in southern Labrador, northern Newfoundland, and on the Southern Shore, but whaling was never a major industry, or an attractive investment for Newfoundland merchant houses. Most of the whaling was done by foreign firms operating in Newfoundland, some of them coming from as far away as Japan. A small inshore whale hunt to produce mink feed flourished in Trinity Bay in the 1960s, but it had only a brief life span, and was virtually dead even before whaling was banned by Canada.

OLD COURT HOUSE AND JAIL, HARBOUR GRACE *(right)*— The cod fishery and the seal hunt were the basis of the great Newfoundland fortunes (and of the prosperity of such mercantile towns as Harbour Grace) in Conception Bay, once described as Newfoundland's "second city." In the nineteenth century the harbours of Carbonear, Harbour Grace, and the Brigus were crammed with shipping. Many vessels hunted seals in the spring, went cod fishing in summer, then sailed to foreign ports with loads of dried and salted cod in autumn. They traded to the West Indies, Brazil, Spain, Portugal, Italy, Greece, and, of course, Great Britain. They brought loads of rum, molasses, salt, dried figs and currants, textiles and shoes, for the merchant houses, but even so had surplus space on their return voyages. Much of the stone that went into such early buildings as this one in Harbour Grace, and into churches and even private houses, was brought from Europe—usually from England—as ballast in the holds of the local ships, to be used by local stone masons. Another source of stone, much used in the walls, paths, and chimneys at Harbour Grace, was nearby Kelly's Island, where thick flagstone that needed no trimming could be loaded in limitless quantities from the beach. Much of the old stonework is still visible in the town today.

OLD ST. PAUL'S, HARBOUR GRACE—This fine stone church, dating from 1835, is typical of the prosperity, buoyancy, and expansion that marked Newfoundland in the period between the end of the War of 1812, and the end of the Boer War (1902). The population of Harbour Grace at mid-century was around five thousand. There was absolutely no unemployment. Indeed, there were too few seamen to man the ships, and too few ships for the trade. Shipbuilding flourished everywhere. Public institutions, churches, government buildings, merchant houses, sprang up everywhere. The offices of the Ridley company were built of stone, to last, like the firm, for centuries. A customs house,

now a museum, opened in 1870. Fraternal organizations such as the Masonic Order and the Benevolent Irish Society built their own elaborate halls. By 1867 the largest Harbour Grace merchant, John Munn and Company, was employing nine thousand people in Newfoundland and Labrador. Main streets were paved with stone and lit by gas. As with many towns of the nineteenth century, fire was a perpetual threat. Most of the waterfront went up in flames in 1832, but was quickly rebuilt. A fire department and pumping engines followed, but there was still no rapid transport to get an engine to the scene of a fire.

GOVERNMENT HOUSE, ST. JOHN'S *(right)*— This substantial stone structure dates from the same period. Previous governors had lived wherever they could—in rented houses, in one of the military forts, even on warships stationed in the harbour. Several of them had urged the British government to build a proper residence for the governor. Thomas Cochrane (governor 1825–1834) finally got his way. Based on plans of the Admiralty House in Plymouth, this building was started in 1827, and occupied while still incomplete in 1831. The house was elaborately furnished with fine imported mahogany, rosewood, carved mantles, as well as Empire gilded mirrors, fine china, and cut glass. Most of

those treasures are still preserved and still in use. Newfoundland's Government House was no architectural gem. The historian D.W. Prowse called it "a huge pile of unredeemed ugliness." But inside it was splendid, and splendidly appointed. At a time of recurrent fish failures, when occasional winters of famine blighted the general prosperity of the country, the select class of St. John's merchants who got to see the inside of this building could well regard it as a symbol of the everlasting mercantile progress in which they so firmly believed, and the divinely established rule of the Queen's government, to which they subscribed.

CAPE SPEAR LIGHTHOUSE (INTERIOR)—The great navigation lights that ring the coast of Newfoundland also date from the period of expansion. The first was built at Fort Amherst in 1810, but the oldest surviving lighthouse is this wooden building at Cape Spear, dating from 1834. Originally it had seven great lenses and reflectors lit by whale oil lamps. James Cantwell, a harbour pilot from St. John's, was made lightkeeper here in 1846 as a reward for rescuing the ship *Rhine* with Prince Henry of the Netherlands. He founded a dynasty of lightkeepers who have tended the Cape Spear light ever since. When the government of Canada built a new lighthouse at Cape Spear, they decided to demolish the original building, but it was saved by a newspaper campaign conducted by the *Evening Telegram* of St. John's, and became part of the Cape Spear National Historic Park. The old lighthouse at Ferryland was also saved by the public after it had already been sold for demolition by the Canadian government. Other fine historic lights are still to be seen at such places as Cape St. Francis and Cape Bonavista. The lenses and lights, marvels of nineteenth-century craftsmanship in brass and glass, came to Newfoundland from Great Britain. Some of them are preserved on the sites, others at the Maritime Museum in the Arts and Culture Centre, St. John's.

FERRYLAND LIGHTHOUSE—This fine nineteenth-century lighthouse on Ferryland Head overlooks one of Newfoundland's most historic harbours, occupied in turn by the pirate admiral Peter Easton, by Lord Baltimore's first colony (1620)—Baltimore built a great house on the neck of Ferryland Head, but no trace of it remains—and by Newfoundland's first royal governor, Sir David Kirke (1638). It was subsequently the scene of many small battles between French naval squadrons and shore batteries built here or on nearby Isle au Bois. Shore batteries were increased and strengthened during the American War of Independence and again at the start of the War of 1812. Many guns and gun emplacements are still to be seen here. The lighthouse was saved from destruction at the last minute by the then Minister of Transport Don Jamieson, on appeal from the Ferryland Historical Society. The contract for its destruction was withdrawn, and the Ferryland Historical Society became its owner. They subsequently made the lighthouse available to artist Gerald Squires as a studio, and he and other artists and craftspeople have made use of it, kept it in repair, and opened it to visitors during the summer months. Other buildings at Ferryland include the school and convent dating from 1858. The church, built of stone from Isle au Bois, was started in 1863.

PITCHER PLANT—One of a number of national symbols, the pitcher plant was chosen by Queen Victoria as Newfoundland's national flower—the sort of gesture at which the Queen Empress was very adept. It was a good choice, a distinctive and very handsome plant ubiquitous in Newfoundland and Labrador. Other national symbols followed. Sir Cavendish Boyle, governor towards the end of Queen Victoria's reign, wrote Newfoundland's national anthem, "The Ode to Newfoundland," which is still sung along with "O Canada" at all public functions. Newfoundland gained Representative Government in 1832 and full Responsible Government in 1855. Newfoundland had her own currency dating from 1834, replacing paper currency previously issued by private merchants. She minted her own coins, beginning in 1865, including such unusual ones as a 20¢ piece, a 5¢ silver coin, and a $2 gold piece. The caribou became Newfoundland's national animal, and a flag bearing a coat of arms far more pictorial than that issued by King Charles I was in general use, though it was never an official national flag. A pink, white, and green flag, equally unofficial, was also flown. Newfoundland brusquely rejected Confederation with Canada when it was proposed in 1867, and vigorously pressed ahead with the business of becoming an independent nation.

HEART'S CONTENT CABLE STATION—The technological revolution began in Newfoundland on July 27, 1866, when the *S.S. Great Eastern* landed the first trans-Atlantic cable at Heart's Content. A few weeks later a second cable, broken and lost in mid-Atlantic the year before, was recovered, spliced, and landed at the same place. Newfoundland thus became the first place in North America to be linked telegraphically to Europe. A cable line was built across the island, and laid under Cabot Strait to link mainland North America with Europe. Heart's Content, a tiny fishing village in the days of the D'Iberville raid, at once became a centre of world communications. The red brick cable station dates from 1873. Its function as a relay centre for international communications declined with the advent of radio and telephone microwave links, until the station was finally closed in 1965. It was subsequently acquired by the Newfoundland government, restored, and stocked with exhibits as a communications museum. The cable brought a small-scale boom to the little fishing hamlet: an influx of new people, roads linking it to other Trinity Bay settlements and across the isthmus to Conception Bay—and, before the boom ended, even a railway and electric power. It was one of the first places in Newfoundland to have a central water supply, a gravity line laid from a lake in the nearby hills by the cable company.

THE INTERIOR BARRENS—For three hundred years after the founding of the fishing stations the interior of Newfoundland remained unexplored. Men ventured up the Exploits as far as Red Indian Lake (usually looking for Indians to rob and murder) and up the Humber to Deer Lake, but the centre of the island, some 30,000 square miles, had never been traversed by a White man, and was reputed to be filled with impassable mountains or impassable swamps or some other figment of the geographical imagination. Those rumours were laid to rest by William Epps Cormack, a St. John's man and citizen of the world who lived in Scotland, Prince Edward Island, Australia, and British Columbia, as well as his native island. On his exploratory journey across Newfoundland in 1822 Cormack was guided by Micmac Indians. He hoped, but failed, to find some surviving Beothuks. What he did find was a vast plateau, filled with lakes that would later produce half a million horsepower of electricity, and river valleys filled to the crests of the hills with forests of spruce, fir, and pine that would support, in turn, a major lumbering industry, and two large paper mills, the first on the Exploits River, the second on the Humber, both in the early years of the twentieth century. An amateur naturalist interested in plants, animals, and minerals, Cormack did much to make possible the opening up of the interior of the country.

BELL ISLAND MINING—In the latter part of the nineteenth century mining suddenly became a major Newfoundland industry. First copper and iron pyrites were mined at various places on the Baie Verte Peninsula—in the beginning at Tilt Cove in 1864, the largest mine being at Bett's Cove, in 1875. In addition to ore, Newfoundland exported smelted copper and copper ingots. By 1877 the value of these exports rose to more than $1.25-million, nearly a fifth of the total exports. The Bell Island ore was known from the earliest times. (John Guy proposed that the London and Bristol Company be granted rights to it.) It was not worked until 1894. Then, very quickly, Bell Island became the biggest iron producer in the British Commonwealth. Later,

Buchans would become an important producer of silver, lead, and zinc concentrates, and would also ship small quantities of copper and gold. Dozens of mines were opened, but most of them had only a short life span, as deposits were exhausted and world demand for ores rose and fell. Bell Island became the major supplier of ore to the smelters at Sydney, Nova Scotia. The deposits were well-nigh inexhaustible, reaching outward for many miles under Conception Bay, but eventually new smelting processes demanded new types of ore, and the Bell Island mines closed in 1966. The island's population of twelve thousand then began to disperse, many to Mainland mining centres.

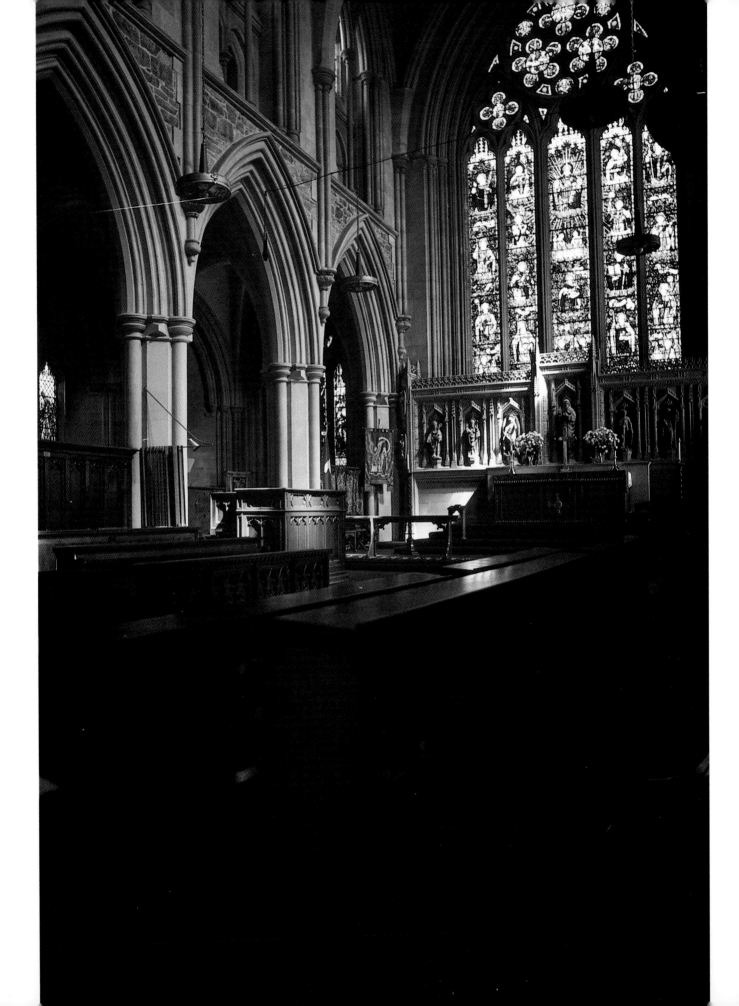

ANGLICAN CATHEDRAL *(left)*—The nineteenth century saw the creation of the architectural monuments that are still the pride of St. John's. The Church of England Cathedral of St. John the Baptist, one of the finest examples of Gothic in the New World, was created by the great Gothic revivalist Sir George Gilbert Scott. The nave was completed and consecrated in 1850, but the transepts and choir were not completed until 1885. In the great fire of 1892, when much of St. John's was destroyed, the Cathedral was all but demolished. The vaulted roof fell in, and all the stained glass, with the exception of the beautiful rose window, disappeared. Rebuilding went on rapidly over the next three years under the direction of Gilbert Scott, son of the original architect. The stained glass was restored—the five towering windows of the west wall being particularly notable. The Cathedral contains many carvings, including a thousand-year-old gargoyle from Bristol, a gift of that city, and a number of Victorian portraits, including that of the Queen and Consort. A small church museum opened here in 1931 contains old photographs, documents, and other relics relating to the history of the parish and of the Church of England in Newfoundland. The Cathedral is the only active parish church in Canada designated a National Historic Site.

BASILICA OF ST. JOHN THE BAPTIST (INTERIOR)—Though not such an architectural gem as the Cathedral, the Basilica has a more richly decorated interior, and is a very impressive building, being, at the time of its creation, the largest church in the New World, north of Mexico. It is designed as a Romanesque cross, 246.5 feet long, 186.5 feet wide. Completed in 1855, it escaped the fire of 1892, and has since been improved with a triple arch at the entrance to the grounds, and with fine marble statuary, both inside the church and on exterior pillars. The altar is especially magnificent, and the carving of the dead Christ is widely regarded as the finest piece of sculpture in the province. The Basilica can seat some eight thousand people. It stands on a hill overlooking the harbour, making it the most imposing landmark in the city. Its grounds are extensive, and include the palace of the Bishop of St. John's, and other church buildings. One of the notable features of the interior is a small shrine with a painted statue of the Virgin, completely out of character with everything else in the Basilica. It was dedicated by Portuguese fishermen from the "white fleet," frequent visitors to St. John's, all of whom had escaped death by storm and shipwreck and chose this means of expressing their thanks.

SQUARE-RIGGED SHIP, ST. JOHN'S—A visitor from Poland, this ship closely resembles many of the ships that carried on Newfoundland's commerce in the nineteenth century. Hundreds of such ships were built, even after the steel shipyards had begun turning out steamships. They not only fished for cod on the Banks and in Labrador, but were the carriers for the seal hunt, and for Newfoundland's foreign and domestic trade. Very few of the outports had any kind of connection by land to the capital or to one another. All intercourse between the hundreds of harbours ringing Newfoundland's coastline was by ship. Ships like this carried the ore and concentrates from Bett's Cove and Tilt Cove, collected and exported fish, and brought all the stocks of the merchant houses from foreign ports. Only slowly were they replaced by tern schooners—mostly smaller, but more manoeuvrable vessels, capable of being worked by smaller crews, and of sailing "closer to the wind" when they had to tack against westerlies, as they usually did on homeward voyages. Even down to the middle years of the twentieth century square-rigged ships were still working in Newfoundland waters, the last of them regularly seen here being the ancient *Gazella*, a hundred-year-old member of the Portuguese fishing fleet that visited St. John's every summer for many years, and during the last years of her active life in the western Atlantic actually survived a hurricane at sea.

THE *KYLE*, STRANDED AT HARBOUR GRACE—Near the end of the nineteenth century, Newfoundland, like many other places, had a great epidemic of railway building. Not only was a line completed all the way across the island to Port aux Basques, but branch lines were opened to the Southern Shore, Conception Bay, Trinity Bay, Placentia Bay, Bonavista, and Lewisporte. Railways were the great economic drive of the time. But the Newfoundland Railway was different from its Mainland cousins. In addition to steam locomotives fired with coal, it owned a large fleet of steel ships, powered by steam heated by bunker. The ships were built in Scotland by some of the finest shipbuilders of their age, and were christened with Scottish names: the *Argyle*, the *Bruce*, the *Clyde*, and so on, through the alphabet. They became the major carriers of all the Newfoundland domestic trade, both freight and passengers, linking St. John's to all the outports, including the settlements along the Labrador coast as far as Nain, and even Hebron. One of the last representatives of this great fleet was the *S.S. Kyle*. She served Labrador and northern Newfoundland for many years, and is remembered in fiction (all the narration of the author's novel *White Eskimo* takes place in one of the *Kyle*'s lounges during a Labrador voyage). She has been rusting away in Harbour Grace since the 1960s.

GRENFELL HOUSE, ST. ANTHONY—Grenfell of Labrador (as he came to be known) was a curious mixture of doctor and evangelist, philanthropist and empire-builder. As a young man he took a medical degree, but also wanted to be a preacher. He eventually managed to combine the two careers by becoming a medical missionary sponsored by the Mission to Deep Sea Fishermen, whose main interest was the distribution of Bibles and religious tracts. He first visited Newfoundland and Labrador in 1892, travelling along the coast as far as Hopedale, distributing literature and medical help to people who had rarely been visited by a doctor. He was a persuasive 'lecturer and fund raiser. In 1893 he returned with two other doctors and two nurses. Soon he had set up his first hospital at Battle Harbour. Later

he made his capital at St. Anthony, in northern Newfoundland, founding a hospital, boarding school, workshops, farm, marine dock, and various other public institutions. He was as interested in social reform, co-operatives, and small industries as he was in religion and medicine, and he did a great deal to bring Newfoundland's "far north" into the social and economic ambit of the country. Grenfell was a very controversial figure, widely disliked, especially by the people whose lives he set out to change, and widely loved, especially by the members of his far-flung organization—the Grenfell Mission, the principal vehicle for social services in the north until after Newfoundland entered Confederation.

Bartlett's cottage, brigus—Captain Bob Bartlett, "the greatest ice navigator of modern times," as Knud Rasmussen called him, was born in Brigus in 1875, when it was already an old merchant town with a great history of seafaring. Bartlett's family included merchant skippers, seal hunters, and ice captains, at least three of whom had made important Arctic voyages in the past. Young Bob was a seal hunter in his father's and uncle's ships, but was too impatient to be a sealing captain. He discovered his true calling in 1898, when he sailed as First Mate with his Uncle John Bartlett on the *Windward*, flagship of Robert Peary's North Pole expedition of that year. Peary was so impressed with the young man that he put him in charge of all his subse-

quent expeditions, and in 1909 Bob Bartlett led a sled expedition that hacked its way through ice ridges and bridged leads of open water to a point 150 statute miles from the pole—the highest confirmed latitude ever reached by anyone in the Arctic before the era of aircraft and air supplies. Peary, who followed Bartlett, later claimed to have gone on from that point to the North Pole. His claim was vigorously disputed, however, and is still highly dubious, because he offered no supporting data, and the sled speeds involved appear to be impossible. Bartlett received, among many other honours, the medal of the Geographical Society of Philadelphia "for discovery of the North Pole," and the Hubbard Medal "for attaining the Farthest North."

IN LOVING MEMORY
OF
WILLIAM JAMES BARTLETT
1851 — 1931.

MARY LEAMON BARTLETT
1852 — 1943.

AND THEIR SON
ROBERT ABRAM BARTLETT
1875 — 1946.

Sɪʀ ᴡɪʟʟɪᴀᴍ ᴄᴏᴀᴋᴇʀ—Few union leaders have wielded such power or reaped such honours as the founder of the first major fishermen's union in Newfoundland. Coaker was never a fisherman. A St. John's boy, he was in turn a merchant's clerk, a telegraph operator, and a farmer in Notre Dame Bay before setting out on a messianic campaign to rescue the fishermen from the toils of the Water Street merchants and their flunkies in the government and legislature. The fishermen followed him in droves. They claimed, at one time, to be "forty thousand strong." They not only joined his union, and subscribed to his Fishermen's Union Trading Company and to many other small companies in which only union members could hold shares, but

they also voted for his candidates, sending eight men to the House of Assembly in 1913. They paraded into the legislature in fishermen's guernseys, outnumbering the Liberals in opposition. From the opposition benches Coaker managed to effect major reforms, including the Sealing Act and the Logging Act, which, for the first time, recognized that workers in those industries had certain rights and must be treated like human beings. Coaker went to the seal hunt as an observer in 1914 to see that the new sealing regulations were followed, and was there at the time of the great *Newfoundland* disaster, when seventy-eight men, separated from their ship, died in a blizzard.

Bᴀʀᴛʟᴇᴛᴛ ᴍᴇᴍᴏʀɪᴀʟ, ʙʀɪɢᴜꜱ(*left*)— *Sails Over Ice*, the title of one of Bartlett's books, is echoed in this memorial to the great explorer who spent his life among the ice floes, and made most of his voyages in sailing ships. After a year or two of glory following the North Pole Expedition of 1909, his fame quickly faded, and he had to take any job he could get so long as it took him back to the far north. He went as captain of the *Karluk*, an ancient barquentine fitted out for the Canadian Arctic Expedition of 1914. He knew she was unfit for the job, and said so, but he went anyway. She was crushed and sunk by ice far to the northwest of Alaska in the middle of the Arctic night. In "the finest example of

leadership in the maritime history of Canada," as the marine historian T. E. Apleton called it, Bartlett managed to lead most of the survivors through a terrible series of pressure ridges to Wrangel Island, and then crossed the running ice to Siberia, where he got word to the outside, and the help of a rescue vessel. Perhaps the most daring and dangerous sledge journey in human history, it won him the Back Grant of the Royal Geographical Society and a gold medal for lifesaving. He later made twenty Arctic voyages in his sailing schooner the *Effie M. Morrissey*, the last one at the age of seventy-five, the year before his death in 1946.

UNION HOUSES, PORT UNION—Coaker created this new town as the centre for his organization's wide-ranging activities. Besides the Fishermen's Union Trading Company, he founded the *Fishermen's Advocate*, a newspaper, as well as a printing company, an export company, a shipbuilding company, and an electric power company, all owned by the union. In 1917 Coaker's Fishermen's Party was taken into a coalition government, but he allowed the merchants to get away with the argument that major reforms must wait until the end of the Great War. He lost much of his support among the fishermen when he voted in favour of conscription—against his own better judgement and stated principles. Nevertheless, in 1919 he and Richard Squires in

coalition carried the country and formed the government. But this alliance with the Liberals proved, in the end, to be a disaster. As Minister of Marine and Fisheries he managed to introduce certain reforms, but failed utterly to create the social revolution of which he had dreamed. The government remained in the hands of merchants and lawyers. The power structure centred in St. John's merely compromised a little, remaining essentially unshaken. He remained in the government, with declining influence, until 1924. In that year he was defeated in the fishing district of Bonavista Bay. Soon afterward he resigned as active head of the union, and eventually retired to Jamaica to enjoy his modest wealth and his knighthood.

FIRST WORLD WAR TRENCH *(right)*— Newfoundland entered the First World War with bugles and shouting, and came out of it bloodied, sickened, and financially damaged. The small country still had a population of less than a quarter of a million people. Most Newfoundlanders had some experience at sea, and recruitment for the Royal Navy alone would have been a reasonable contribution to the British Empire's war effort. Instead, the government decided to allow as many as wished to do so to volunteer for the navy, and in addition to raise and equip an infantry regiment. In a series of suicidal battles on the Western Front the Royal Newfoundland Regiment covered itself with glory and bled itself white. The worst of several disasters was at the

opening of the Battle of the Somme, when the Newfoundlanders were ordered by incompetent commanders to make a bayonet charge from their trenches against German machine gun positions. They were slaughtered in No Man's Land without getting close to the German lines. On the day after the Beaumont-Hammel disaster only 68 men out of a regiment of more than 1,000 could be mustered for duty. In April 1917 the regiment suffered 460 casualties in the Battle of Arras. At Poelcappelle in October, 194 were lost, and at Cambrai in December, 319. Following this series of suicide missions, the King awarded the regiment the title "Royal," the only regiment to receive the honour in the First World War.

CARIBOU HEAD—Cast in bronze at Bowring Park, near St. John's, the caribou is one of many war memorials throughout the island. The caribou head was the badge of the Royal Newfoundland Regiment, and was later carried on many Newfoundland stamps. The war entered very deeply into the consciousness of the people. There were casualties in the navy, in the merchant marine, and among Newfoundlanders in allied forces, but the disasters on the Western Front touched almost everyone in the country. Scarcely a family escaped the loss of some of its young men. Two Newfoundlanders won the Victoria Cross. But the regiment had suffered 3,619 casualties, 1,305 of them killed in action. In addition, 180 of the 2,000 volunteers in the navy were killed. There were also civilian deaths—three in the Newfoundland Forestry Corps of 500, and merchant seamen who have not been included in any total of war casualties. The casualty rate among Newfoundlanders was said to be the highest in the British Empire. In spite of all this there was a great feeling of pride in the way they went to their deaths. Captain Leo Murphy probably echoed a national sentiment when he described the suicidal advance at Beaumont-Hammel as the finest sight he had ever witnessed. Nevertheless, by 1917 there was beginning to be strong resistance to the recruiting drives, and the government felt compelled to turn to conscription to keep the regiment supplied with bodies.

GAS MASK, MILITARY MUSEUM, ST. JOHN'S *(right)*— The Newfoundlanders first came under gas attack from the German army in 1917, almost two years after the first clouds of chlorine had drifted down on the Canadian trenches at Ypres. Meanwhile the gas mask had been invented by a young Newfoundland medical officer, Lieutenant-Colonel Cluny MacPherson of St. John's, and the entire British army had been equipped with his gas helmets. These were fully effective against chlorine, which killed and disabled only when it was inhaled, but were only partly effective against mustard gas, used later, a substance that could cause severe burns on contact. MacPherson's gas mask was replaced, later in the war, by the muzzle-like box respirator that is familiar in pictures of trench warfare from 1917 and 1918. Meanwhile, the strategy of using poison gas as a weapon had proved ineffective. After the initial psychological shock was over it proved to be far less potent than high explosives and machine gun bullets, and has never been used extensively in warfare in recent times. Conscription, intended to reinforce the decimated ranks of the Royal Newfoundland Regiment, became law in 1918. But most of the men left in Newfoundland were medically unfit—only 1,573 out of 3,629 could meet the very low health standards required. No conscript ever reached the front. They were still in training when the war ended November 11, 1918.

CAPTAIN COOK MEMORIAL—The optimism of the 1920s was not altogether unfounded. The Humber, previously the domain of lobstermen, herring packers, a few trappers, and a small sawmill industry, became the centre of a great economic development. Unlike the east coast, Bay of Islands and the Humber region had a comparatively short history. A French fishing preserve, home to a few Micmac Indians and even fewer settlers, little was known about it until the arrival of Captain James Cook, who began a comprehensive survey of the coasts of Newfoundland in 1763, and completed the work in 1767, so thoroughly that his charts still form the basis of those in use today. He observed and reported an eclipse of the sun at Burgeo.

Cook was much impressed by the resources of the west coast—by coal beds that he saw near St. George's and by the forest and waterpower of the Humber. His glowing reports brought no immediate action from the colonial authorities, but were not forgotten. A century and a half after his time they were read by a Newfoundland business man, W. D. Reid, who happened to own vast tracts of land in central and western Newfoundland acquired during the building of the railway. Reid was firmly convinced that forests, minerals, and waterpower could all be combined to turn the Humber Valley into an industrial centre far greater than the Grand Falls development on the Exploits.

WAR MEMORIAL, ST. JOHN'S *(left)*— The government had borrowed $13-million to finance the war. Along with other expensive undertakings such as the railway, and especially the money-losing branch lines, this raised the national debt by 1920 to $43-million, five times higher than the annual revenue. Wartime prosperity vanished. Fish markets collapsed. Annual deficits ran to four or five million dollars, and the government began borrowing to pay the interest on its loan. But in the midst of widespread unemployment and depressed fishing and mining industries there was great optimism. The paper mill on the Exploits was a great success. Others were sure to follow, on the Humber and the Gander. Within four years the government had collapsed in

a welter of graft and corruption, but even this did not dim the optimism of the 1920s. This splendid National War Memorial was unveiled in 1924 by Field Marshal Earl Haig, who had been British Commander-in-Chief. Standing on King's Beach, where Sir Humphrey Gilbert proclaimed the first British rule in North America, it is surmounted by the bronze figure of Freedom, with sword and torch, with figures below representing the Royal Newfoundland Regiment, the Naval Reserve, the Merchant Marine, and the Forestry Corps. Memorial University College (later Memorial University of Newfoundland) was also founded as a tribute to the country's war dead.

Logs, CORNER BROOK—Forestry developed slowly in Humber Valley. A Canadian with the incredible name of Gay Silver owned a sawmill at Corner Brook as early as 1864. The mill was later bought by Christopher Fisher, and enlarged. The Fisher property was eventually sold to become the site of the paper mill, but the sawmill continued operating at the place where Corner Brook stream enters Humber Arm until it was closed by the Great Depression in the mid-1930s. W. D. Reid's promotions attracted other business interests, and the attention of the Newfoundland government, especially of Prime Minister Richard Squires, who made the Humber development a major plank in his election platforms, and helped to attract British interests. In combination with Reid they formed the Newfoundland Power and Paper Company in 1923, and began that year the construction of a paper mill at Corner Brook and a power plant at Deer Lake. The whole project was carried through with incredible speed. By 1924 the first paper was produced, and by 1925 the mill was in full production. The construction created a temporary employment boom, and the mill, once in operation, was a centre of prosperity, and focus for a logging industry that extended north and south of Bay of Islands and up Humber Valley deep into the interior. "Putting the hum in the Humber" had amply fulfilled its promise.

CORNER BROOK MILL—The company that built the mill at Corner Brook did not have the financial resources to operate it for long. After two years they sold it to the International Paper Company of New York. This company enlarged both the paper mill and the power plant, speeded up the machines, and hired larger crews. But eventually world depression overtook them and the mill went on short time, lost money, and was bought at a bargain by Bowaters of England, in 1938. From that time the Corner Brook mill flourished exceedingly, and was enlarged still further until it became the world's largest producer of paper, with an output greater than a thousand tons of newsprint a day. Pulp for export was also produced. Besides creating a prosperous city on Newfoundland's west coast, the Corner Brook mill was immensely profitable to its owners. It was the foundation of the far-ranging Bowater empire in North America, and it was not uncommon for it to return a net profit on the order of $50-million a year. But the industry had its ups and downs, following shifts in world demand for newsprint. During one of the downs in the 1960s, Bowaters tried to sell the mill, but found no buyer. In the 1970s it produced profits measured in the hundreds of millions. Then, in the 1980s, during another recession, they announced the mill would be sold or closed. It was purchased by the Kruger corporation to run on a reduced basis, and Corner Brook's greatest days seemed to be over.

THE ATLANTIC FLIGHTS—This monument at Harbour Grace commemorates the series of Atlantic crossings that pioneer fliers made in the 1920s and 1930s. Because Newfoundland was the closest part of North America to Europe, it was a favoured departure point, and that was why Harbour Grace built North America's first commercial airport in 1927. The first non-stop crossing of the Atlantic had been made in 1919 by John Alcock and Arthur Brown flying from St. John's to Ireland in a twin-engined Vickers Vimy bomber converted for long-range flight. More than twenty such flights were attempted from Harbour Grace, many of them successful, though some of the Atlantic fliers were fished out of the sea, and others vanished without a trace. Among the famous people who flew out of Harbour Grace were Charles Edward Kingsford-Smith in 1930 (first to fly around the world), Amelia Earhart in 1932 (first woman to fly the Atlantic solo), and the World War ace Captain Eddie Rickenbacker, in 1936. The last Atlantic crossing by a light aircraft from Harbour Grace was made in October 1936, after which the airstrip built specifically for such use went into mothballs until the Second World War, when it was reactivated for anti-submarine work.

Job barbour and *Neptune II*—An unintentional Atlantic crossing was made in 1929 by a Newfoundland coastal skipper, his passengers, and crew, in a small vessel, the *Neptune II*, that blew away from the coast in a gale. Captain Job Barbour had no navigation equipment and little fresh water on his vessel. After three days of storm he had no idea how to get back to Newfoundland, and no clear notion of where he was going, except that he was drifting in a generally easterly direction. When he sighted land after forty-eight days adrift, he feared that it might be some savage part of Africa where he and his companions would be eaten by cannibals. It turned out to be Scotland, and Barbour came home to write a book that entertained many and angered professional sailors. Eventually it went into a second edition, and *Forty-Eight Days Adrift* became a Newfoundland legend. Barbour obtained, in Great Britain, an agency for marine engines, and succeeded in business far better than he had as a mariner. His small company weathered the Great Depression, and he remained active in business long after Newfoundland entered Confederation.

BEAU BOIS AND BAY L'ARGENT—The Great Depression of the 1930s hit Newfoundland very hard. Markets for fish, paper, and minerals almost disappeared, and little settlements like these, which had been self-sufficient for centuries, suddenly found themselves with no income other than the meagre "dole" passed out by the government to ward off absolute starvation. Outport Newfoundlanders were not hit quite so hard as people in single-crop regions such as the Prairies and the American Plains. If you lived beside the sea, no matter how poor you were, you could usually cure enough fish for your own use. The nearby woods provided some meat: a poached moose or a few brace of rabbits caught in

wire snares. There were usually good crops of berries on the high ground, and a family could pick more berries than they could find the sugar to preserve. The more self-sufficient people who had always done some gardening continued to do so. Anyone with a plot of ground could grow enough potatoes and turnips for a year. But some of the fishing settlements were literally built on rocks, and had no tradition of gardening. In a few places cod fish was as much a "one-crop economy" as wheat was on the Prairies. To alleviate distress and give people something to do, the government began evacuating them to "land settlements," where more or less fertile soil had been cleared by govern-

ment machinery, and small houses were built to replace those abandoned in the fishing settlements. The weakness of the plan was that those most in need were precisely those who had no tradition of working the soil. As a direct result of the Depression the government found itself facing bankruptcy, no longer able to raise the revenue to pay the interest on its loans—which, in any case, had been mounting recklessly for years past. In the crisis, the government appealed to Great Britain, and gave up its status as a self-governing Dominion. Newfoundland did not revert to a Crown colony, but became a Dominion with suspended constitution, ruled by an appointed Commission Government consisting of an appointed governor as chairman, and six commissioners, three from Newfoundland and three from England. The arrangement was highly successful. The Commission put the public finances on a sound basis, strengthened the economy with land settlements and expanded forest industries, and began converting the fishery to a fresh-frozen pack for which the market was strong. By 1938 they had pulled Newfoundland up by its own bootstraps, and the Depression was ending earlier than in most parts of North America.

SCHOONER *MARJORIE N. INKPEN*—Throughout the 1930s, most of the Newfoundland trade was carried in schooners such as the *Marjorie N. Inkpen*, owned by Captain George H. Blackwood, built in Shelburne, Nova Scotia, in 1911. Some of them were owned by large St. John's merchant houses, the Crosbies, the Munroes, the Hickmans, Baine Johnston and Company, Job Brothers. They used the schooners not only to carry their foreign trade, but also to supply branch stores throughout the island and along the coast of Labrador, and to collect fish for their central warehouses in St. John's. Even more important to the life of the outports was a host of smaller vessels owned by independent outport merchants like the Keans and Barbours of Bonavista Bay, the Holletts of Burin, the Penneys of Ramea. Owners of single schooners often sailed their own vessels,

itinerant traders taking whatever freights offered, and also carrying passengers at very low rates to and from all the tiny fishing harbours that ringed the coast of Newfoundland. There were about nine hundred places[†] in Newfoundland permanently inhabited at one time or another, all of them requiring communications by sea. The number of inhabited harbours and coves began to decline as some of them were abandoned during the Depression, and declined further some years later, when "centralization" became government policy. A modern map will list about six hundred cities, towns, and settlements.

[†] This is my own estimate, using maps, but some estimates put the number at more than one thousand.

FISHERMAN'S BOOTS—The green door is typical of outport taste in house decoration. Many people paint their houses in three bright colours, even in bands, one above the another. Despite the growth of the forest industries and new mines at Buchans and St. Lawrence, the fishery remained by far the largest employer and the mainstay of the Newfoundland economy. There really were some forty thousand fishermen in Coaker's time, and even with the "rationalization" of the industry that came with the building of the freezer plants and the coming of the offshore draggers, the number of fishermen remained above thirty thousand. Many fishermen worked as loggers during the winter, but fishing remained at the centre of their lives, even when it produced little income, until the enormous demand for construction workers in the 1940s took thousands of them out of their boats, leaving, in many cases, boats and gear to deteriorate until they became unusable and unrepairable.

THE DORY—This flat-bottomed row boat, pointed at both ends and with flaring sides, is said to be the most seaworthy small boat ever designed. It was used by banking schooners because of its seaworthiness, the men who fished with hand trawls on the banks being forced to work long distances from their ships, often in bad weather. The dory floated on top of the water, like a cork. It tossed and knocked about frightfully in a sea, but tended not to ship water or overturn. It happened, also, to be a design that could be nested, in stacks, on a banking schooner's deck. Dories were usually worked by two-man crews, though lone fishermen sometimes used them for inshore work. Until a generation or two ago, the dory was almost exclusively found along the south coast of Newfoundland. The more populous northeast coast preferred the trap skiff and the "rodney"—a round-bottomed row boat of more conventional design. But the dory is such a practical boat, easy to build, easy to haul up a slipway, adaptable to an inboard-outboard motor, as well as to oars and even a sail, that it is now popular in all parts of the province.

THE REGATTA—Nothing ever dampened the Newfoundlanders' love of fun and sport. The annual regatta at Quidi Vidi Lake, St. John's, was as big an institution throughout the years of the Depression as it had been since it was first held in 1828. Said to be the oldest annual sporting event in North America, it was also perhaps the only sporting event to be the excuse for a national holiday—a movable feast held on the first Wednesday in August, or on the first suitable day thereafter when the all-powerful Regatta Committee decreed that wind and weather were right for the great event at the lake. It wasn't just boat races. It was a carnival, a side-show, with games of chance, games of skill, brass bands playing, spruce beer foaming from newly opened bottles, food served out of tents, and races in eight-oared shells ending in the grand climax of the championship race of the year. But the fastest time of the day was rarely made in the championship race. Who could contain his thirst for spruce beer until the evening? Besides, there was the wonderful record time for the course set in 1901 by the Outercove Fishermen—a record that stood for three quarters of a century before it was finally beaten. Tradition? The Regatta *was* Newfoundland. Crowds of up to forty-thousand turned out for the event.

GUN EMPLACEMENTS, FORT AMHERST—These shore defences date from the Second World War when Cape Spear, and the old forts at St. John's harbour, were armed once again as defence against merchant raiders and submarines. From 1939 to 1943 Newfoundland was besieged by submarines. They closed the St. Lawrence River and almost succeeded in closing the Strait of Belle Isle. They sank the big Newfoundland ferry *Caribou*, which connected Port aux Basques with North Sydney, and in two separate attacks at Bell Island they sank four ore carriers and blew up the loading pier. Newfoundland had carried out the first act of war in North America by seizing ships in her ports immediately war was declared on September 3, 1939. The Commission Government, with its usual prudence, decided not to repeat the bloodbath and the economic burden that Newfoundland had endured in the First World War. Two artillery regiments were raised from Newfoundland volunteers. Their tasks would be less dangerous than that of infantry regiments. And Newfoundland was not asked to undertake the expense of equipping them. Instead, Newfoundland made interest-free loans to Britain, and Newfoundlanders were encouraged to contribute both by gifts of fighter aircraft and by war savings bonds. Large numbers also served in the navy, air force, and merchant marine, where casualties were much heavier than in the previous war. The Newfoundland regiments fought in Africa, Sicily, Italy, and in the invasion of Normandy.

Hᴜᴅꜱᴏɴ ʙᴏᴍʙᴇʀ, ꜰᴇʀʀʏ ᴄᴏᴍᴍᴀɴᴅ—With remarkable foresight, the government of Newfoundland began work on Gander Airport in 1937, and had the runways open early in 1938. Gander became a major base for military operations in the Second World War. It was the departure point for aircraft of the Ferry Command, an organization set up to fly military aircraft across the Atlantic from North America, where they were being manufactured, to Great Britain, where they could fight the war. They took off from Gander in a continuous stream, to reinforce the Royal Air Force. At one point the aircraft of the Ferry Command were taking to the air at the rate of one plane every sixty seconds. A large air base was later built at Goose Bay in Labrador, and beginning in 1940 the American armed forces built bases at Fort Pepperell in St. John's (later headquarters of the Northeast Air Command), at Stephenville on the west coast, and at Argentia in the south. Stephenville was an air force base and Argentia a naval base. Planes from both bases were engaged in the Battle of the Atlantic. St. John's became an armed camp during the war, with Newfoundland, Canadian, and American servicemen all stationed in the vicinity. Relations between these allies were often far from cordial. To lessen the submarine menace, a blackout was imposed, and blacked-out towns and cities inhabited by restless servicemen and gangs of construction workers became centres of continual violence.

JOEY—Union organizer, newspaper reporter, broadcaster, hog farmer, Joseph R. Smallwood came crashing onto the political scene in 1946, determined to change the history of his native island. That was the year Great Britain decided Newfoundland should hold a referendum on its future form of government. Without Smallwood the result would have been a foregone conclusion. Newfoundland would have reverted to being a self-governing Dominion, and the politics of the 1920s would have returned. Smallwood, the ablest and most persuasive politician in Newfoundland history, decided on Confederation with Canada, created an organization to bring it about, and within three years was the first Premier of the province of Newfoundland. He believed he was a socialist, but embraced the Liberal Party from expediency, and kept it in power in Newfoundland for twenty-two years and nine months, the longest unbroken run any Newfoundland politician has ever enjoyed before or since. Having changed his country's political history, he set out to change its economic structure. To Smallwood "economic development" meant factories. He struggled desperately to get Newfoundlanders out of their fishing boats and into the production lines. It became government policy to close down the fishing settlements and move people to "growth centres," where economic development was to follow.

BARKING KETTLE FLOWER POT—One of the symbols of the Newfoundland outports for centuries, the barking kettle was used to steep fishing nets in a hot infusion of bark, the tannin of which acted as a preservative against rot. Barking the nets was a community effort, carried out by all the fishermen of a harbour before the fishing season started. One-half of Smallwood's centralization policy succeeded. Thousands of people from hundreds of settlements quit fishing and moved to growth centres, but in most cases the growth centres turned out to be welfare centres. The only places where centralization succeeded, economically, were at those few growth centres where there was a flourishing fishing industry. Most of the small factories opened in Smallwood's era of economic development quickly failed.

Most of the really grand schemes never materialized. Those that did, failed too, sooner or later. A few small developments—a cement mill and gypsum plant at Corner Brook for instance—succeeded, but the overall effect on the economy of the province was slight. Even the massive hydroelectric development at Churchill Falls turned out to be of great benefit to Quebec, and of very little benefit to Newfoundland. New mines opened. The iron mines in western Labrador produced a new population centre far more prosperous and attractive than Bell Island had ever been. But the economy of the island of Newfoundland changed little. Despite this, Smallwood, a gentleman farmer, told a royal commission: "The cowboy looms larger than the fisherman in Newfoundland's future."

PORT AUX BASQUES FERRY—The big plus for Newfoundland was social capital, rather than direct economic development. Under the terms of Confederation, which came into effect March 31, 1949, Canada provided a motor ferry link between Newfoundland and Nova Scotia. Eventually three and even four large ferries would be required to carry the traffic. The Trans-Canada Highway in Newfoundland, built mainly with federal funds, and completed by 1965, did more for the economic life of the province than all the factories built by Newfoundland government guarantees. Almost in the year of its completion young Newfoundland-ers became travellers. Young people who had never before been fifty miles from home were suddenly at home in every city on the continent. Many of them returned with the conviction that the best things of all were in Newfoundland itself: the folklore, the music, the folk art that had flourished in the island right from the days of the Cupids Colony when the rest of North America was an unsettled wilderness without the smallest pretension to culture of any kind. They created a great boom in "Newf-Cult" and spread it far beyond the borders of their own province.

CHRIS AND MARY PRATT'S KITCHEN—Among the major exponents of Newf-Cult are Christopher and Mary Pratt, magic realist artists formerly of Salmonier, now of St. John's. Their subjects are Newfoundland, often Newfoundland archetypes. Their styles, radically different, though in both cases squarely in the magic realist mode, appeal equally to those educated in art, and to those who couldn't tell a Picasso from an El Greco. In addition to visual art, the great Newfoundland renaissance has included theatre, especially satirical and social theatre, popular music, folk revivals of all kinds, and a great spate of literature, including imaginative prose and contemporary poetry. By the 1980s there were four substantial publishing houses at St. John's, all of them dealing mainly, though not exclusively, in Newfoundland materials. Several of the most successful Newfoundland artists chose to live in other parts of Canada, but others, equally successful, chose to stay at home. In previous generations they would have migrated to the United States or Great Britain. People of the Pratts' generation proved, for the first time, that you could make a success while living at Salmonier, Beachy Cove, or in a lighthouse on Ferryland Head.

BOYS JIGGING CONNERS—The return to the sea was simply going home for Newfoundlanders. They'd loved it, hated it, but always lived with it, they and their ancestors since men began to eat fish. Newfoundland boys spend their leisure time on wharf heads and in boats. When the ice drives into the harbours in pans that will bear your weight for a few moments before they begin to sink, they go "copying" over the ice, falling in, hauling each other out. A business man who sold his bus line to return to fishing in the stormy little cove of Bauline said, "There've been times, coming in to that slipway, when I wouldn't give two cents for my life. But I went back to it just the same." A bus line might earn

him more money, but a fishing boat was home. Since fishing became economically feasible in the 1960s, there has never been any real question of Newfoundlanders becoming cowboys or production line workers. A few of them might work on oil rigs, or in other parts of the oil industry, just as some had become papermakers and airline pilots, but for the vast majority real life consists in working alone or in small groups in boats or small ships, making sure they simply keep abreast of the technology and protect the fish stocks. That, however, is a very big challenge indeed—perhaps the biggest one facing any Newfoundland government of the future.

FISHERMEN WITH NETS *(left)*— The 1960s saw not only the birth of Newf-Cult and Newfoundlanders for the first time near the leading edge of international culture, but also a massive return to the very basis of the whole Newfoundland tradition. The fisheries were revived largely by the extension of unemployment insurance to the fishing occupations. Once started, the revival proceeded on its own. New species such as crab became important. Public taste began to accept fish not as a substitute for meat, but as a luxury food. New or at least almost new technology made the fisherman's task a great deal easier than it had been in his father's time. A powerful union, with none of the built-

in weaknesses that had killed Coaker's union, saw to it that the fisherman got a reasonable share of the profits of the industry. At the dawn of the 1980s the Newfoundland fishermen were no longer at the bottom of the heap, the poorest class in the island. In addition to hundreds of thousands of dollars in boats and gear, a fisherman might now own a modern home with colour TV and a new car (or two) and might be worried about income tax auditors breathing down his neck. Fish failures would still threaten ruin in some years, but in good years fishermen lived lives at least as comfortable as those of the merchants in their grandparents' time.

BAKEAPPLES AND NATIONAL PARKS—The federal presence in Newfoundland created havens of a special heritage that might otherwise have been lost. The two national parks—first Terra Nova, later Gros Mourne—were created with great misgiving, and after a struggle of ideologies. The idea of setting aside large tracts of land with all their resources to be preserved for the pleasure and education of the public was completely foreign to a government hell-bent on "development." In the words of a provincial minister of resources, they needed "every stick for pulp." The bait of thirty miles of paved highway built entirely at federal expense made Terra Nova a reality. Later, massive public pressure created the great scenic and wildlife preserve of Gros Mourne, despite the hungry maws of the pulp machines and the government's nearly hysterical fear that it might be "giving away a mine" of silica rock that could be processed into glass. The humble and beautiful bakeapple, here preserved for the future, is Newfoundland's national fruit, a universal favourite with Newfoundlanders at home and abroad. If you want to make an expatriate weep for joy, you send him a jar of bakeapple jam. Many other plants, from lovely bog orchids to noble white pines, share the refuge of the national parks with moose and caribou, bald eagles, shy pine martens, and bold arctic hares.

Scenic gros mourne—One of the great national parks of Canada, Gros Mourne is a splendid series of cliffs and gorges—some of them 2,500 feet deep—cut by lovely salt water fjords, and a great tableland, sub-arctic in nature, lying above. The Long Range Mountains in this park date from one-and-a-half *billion* years ago, three times older than the mountains of New England and Gaspé. Worn down by all the ice ages that the earth has ever known, they are massive brooding presences, totally unlike the young, rugged peaks of the Rockies or the Cascades. The lowlands have their own beauty. Woodland glades glow with yellow lady's slippers and purple moccasin flowers. The drier boglands are blankets of silver-white or orange-bronze cotton grass. The dry ridges blaze with arctic rhododendron in great banks of purple-red, more strongly massed than similar flowers farther south. Low-lying pools and streams carry equally dense masses of blue flag iris, a greater show of this striking flower than is ever seen in more southerly parts of North America. And always, along the western shore, are the beaches, including raised beaches from inter-glacial eras of the past, great stretches of sand dunes, and massive folds of rock, with the waters of the Gulf of St. Lawrence murmuring or roaring below. If you follow the road through the park and on to St. Barbe Bay, you eventually reach a ferry that will take you to Labrador.

TERRA NOVA PARK—Set in the loveliest part of historic Bonavista Bay, Terra Nova National Park includes the waters of Sweet Bay, Newman's Sound, and Clode Sound—some of the finest boating and yachting waters of eastern Canada—as well as salmon rivers and large up-country lakes in a stretch of spruce forest that seems to be positively swarming with moose, black bear, and other animals of the boreal zone. Moose often can be photographed at the roadside, grazing like domestic cattle. Bears are common enough to be regarded as a nuisance. There have been no bear attacks reported from Terra Nova, but visitors are advised to keep their distance all the same. Pictures are best taken from a car with telephoto lens. Terra Nova is an excellent place for sea birds—not only such common ones as gulls and terns and numerous species of ducks, but also such handsome migrants as turnstones, dowitchers, golden plovers, and curlews. Indeed, a dedicated bird-watcher can easily run up a list of fifty maritime species in Terra Nova, and fifty others from the adjoining forests and boglands. The park includes all facilities for visitors by boat as well as by car or camper. One of Newfoundland's best canoe routes lies through the waters of Sweet Bay and Alexander Bay and the nearby Terra Nova River.

MARYSTOWN SHIPYARD—With the discovery of the Newfoundland heritage in fishing villages and wilderness, and the return to the fishery, came new industries also based on tradition. Shipbuilders have been important in Newfoundland at least from the time of Frontenac. By the later years of the twentieth century steel shipbuilding was at last beginning to be an important industry. There were shipyards at St. John's, Harbour Grace, and Marystown, as well as small shipyards for building wooden draggers in other places. By the 1980s the Marystown shipyard was not only building steel draggers for offshore fishing, but had also developed such sophisticated technology that it could build oil-drilling ships. Among customers for such products was Norway, which placed orders in Marystown for drilling ships to be used on the North Sea oilfields. The Marystown ships were equipped with computers and specialized location equipment that enabled them to hold station over any selected patch of sea bottom within a tolerance of less than one metre. The ships were scientific tools of great precision, doing a job of location and discovery more fundamental than that of the drilling rigs. Marystown is just one of Newfoundland's historic towns that has begun a leap into a new age with the oil boom.

St. john's—This town, Canada's oldest provincial capital by at least one hundred years, now looks over a past that ranges backward for nearly half a millennium, and into a future that appears to be golden with oil. The discoveries on the continental shelf off Newfoundland are indeed massive ones, and will be developed, sooner or later. By 1985 a prolonged wrangle between the federal and provincial governments over who owned the oil was at last settled, and it was assured that the Newfoundland government, the Newfoundland people, and the people and government of Canada, would all benefit fairly from the offshore oil when the development reached the stage of production, be that soon or late. Meanwhile there was a positive anxiety to preserve the past in St. John's, and to restore its downtown core to something resembling its Victorian beauty. Some unfortunate highrise buildings were permitted on the waterfront, but there was such a popular revulsion against this trend that it did not go very far. Downtown St. John's still looks more like a European than a North American city, and it now seems to be assured that the character of the city, created over such a long period by fishing masters and merchants from the west of England, will be preserved for the foreseeable future.

CHIMNEY POT—One of a thousand ceramic chimney pots that help to give St. John's its character. Other elements from the past of this unique city include stone crosswalks, and stone or concrete flights of stairs between streets. Many houses boast elaborate Victorian entrances, often with decorations of Victorian stained glass. Turned wooden posts and wooden decorations on gables and eaves are very common. There are numerous wrought-iron fences from an era in which such fences were the ultimate status symbol. All of this was in danger of destruction just a few years ago, but is now being preserved by a people fully conscious of the richness of their past.

Coastal scene with mist—Governor Sir Cavendish Boyle expressed it for all time back in 1901:

When sun-rays crown thy pine-clad hills
And summer spreads her hand,
When silvern voices tune thy rills,
We love thee, smiling land....

When spreads thy cloak of shimmering white
At winter's stern command;
Through shortened day and star-lit night
We love thee, frozen land....

As loved our fathers so we love,
Where once they stood, we stand;
Their prayer we raise to heaven above,
God guard thee, Newfoundland.